Katharina Schlegl-Kofler

Educating Your Dog
with Love and Understanding

The basics of appropriate training for all dogs, from puppyhood through adulthood

Color photos by Christine Steimer

Drawings by Renate Holzner

Consulting Editor:
  Matthew M. Vriends, Ph.D.

Translated from the German by
  Elizabeth D. Crawford

BARRON'S

Contents

By lowering its forequarters to the ground, this dog is issuing an invitation to play.

Preface

Training is extremely important if your dog is to develop its abilities to the utmost. It will give your pet a sense of security and a greater degree of freedom.

Modern methods of dog training use the dog's natural patterns of behavior to advantage. The exercises are fun to learn, and your pet will participate enthusiastically in the training sessions. This gentle approach to training respects the dog's personality but makes the animal into an obedient companion. In the HOW-TO sections of this new Complete Pet Owner's Manual, Katharina Schlegl-Kofler presents training programs for both puppies and fully grown dogs.

The individual exercises are explained step by step, and you can easily teach your pet to perform them—even if you are a novice in handling a dog.

The exercise portion of this manual concludes with a training plan that offers a great deal of variety. The author also shows what influence the wolf's legacy has on the dog, and what you, as a dog owner, can learn from that. In the individual phases of its development a puppy establishes, through repetition, patterns that will determine its behavior throughout its life. This book tells you what to pay attention to during these sensitive periods. In the chapter Basic Course for Trainers, the author presents a number of important training rules.

The author of this book and the editors of Barron's series of pet manuals wish you a great deal of pleasure as you successfully train your dog.

Please read the Important Note on page 63.

3

Why Training Your Dog Is Important

Dogs, Then and Now

We humans have treasured the companionship of dogs for some ten thousand years.

In earlier times the dog served as a helper in the hunt, a protector of sheep and cattle herds, and a guardian of house and home. Over the centuries, the dog's place changed more and more. Today, most dog owners view their pet mainly as a companion in leisure activities and a beloved member of their household.

Whether an expensive purebred or a mixed breed, the dog has become the most popular of the domestic animals, probably because no other domestic animal is capable of forming such a close relationship with a human.

Nevertheless, every dog, big or small, needs care and training in keeping with the requirements of its breed. Only then can a genuinely harmonious relationship develop between a dog and its owner.

Today especially, many people and fairly large numbers of dogs live in densely populated areas. If your pet is to avoid being a nuisance to anyone and endangering either itself or others, it has to learn certain rules, to make it better able to get along in our civilized world.

Spending a great deal of time in activities with your dog also contributes to the strength of the bond between you and your pet and ensures that your companion stays mentally fit. It is true, however, that training a dog properly is time consuming; it is not comparable to keeping a guinea pig, for instance. Every would-be dog owner needs to be aware of that point.

Which Dog Is Right for You?

You're interested in acquiring a dog. If you want a purebred, you have the problem of deciding on one of almost 400 different dog breeds. Which breed suits you best? Before you buy, consider these points:

• To live together in harmony, it is important that owner and dog be right for each other. Someone who tends to be sedentary and is not athletically inclined should not own a setter or a Dalmatian, and a Doberman pinscher is not the best choice for a couch potato. These are serious mismatches. You also need to be aware that not all small dog breeds make good lap dogs, however cute they may look.

• Make a list of the traits you expect the new member of the family to possess. Do you want the dog to accompany you on bicycle trips and mountain hikes? Do you want it to be primarily a family pet or a watchdog? Does your family include small children (see page 58)? These are just a few examples.

• Don't select a breed just because you like the way it looks or, possibly, because it is "in" at the moment! Trendy breeds and breeds that for many years were bred only for beauty often exhibit signs of degeneration with regard to their character and health.

Acquiring a dog is a step you should consider very carefully. With dogs, as opposed to other pets, proper training is of enormous importance. It requires a great deal of time, patience, and consistency on the dog owner's part.

A well-trained dog doesn't need to be on leash when it waits in front of a store.

The puppy will thoroughly investigate everything in its new home, but, from the very beginning, you should forbid your puppy to chew on rugs.

How to Find the Right Breeder

Once you have selected a particular breed, allow yourself plenty of time to search for a suitable breeder.

It is best to contact the American Kennel Club (AKC; see Useful Addresses, page 62) for the addresses of reputable breed clubs in this country. The umbrella organization for the dog breed associations elsewhere in the world is the Fédération Cynologique Internationale (FCI). Only dogs from breeders affiliated with these authorities are internationally recognized and have a corresponding notation in their pedigree.

Since the AKC lays down strict ground rules for all its member clubs, it offers you the best guarantee of getting a healthy dog that is a typical representative of its breed.

Note: If, later on, you would like to participate with your purebred dog in breed-specific training courses and examinations or shows, your dog generally will be accepted only if it comes from a breeder with AKC membership.

My tip: A visit to a national or international dog show is a good opportunity to obtain information about dog breeds. You can find out from the AKC when and where shows are held.

What to Look for When Choosing a Puppy

The strongest bond and the most successful basic and advanced training can be achieved if the dog comes to its new owner as a puppy.

The first eight to 12 weeks of the puppy's life are spent at the breeder's. This period is of fundamental importance in its life. It will affect the remainder of the dog's life as well as its participation in its human pack. When buying a puppy, therefore, keep these things in mind:

1. Buy only from reputable breeders, never from dog dealers who have only puppies and no breeding stock.

2. Make sure that the breeder breeds no more than one or two breeds and does not offer a host of different breeds for sale.

3. It is important that you be able to see the mother dog for yourself. Never buy a puppy if that is not possible.

4. A good breeder does not own too many dogs and raises only one or two litters at a time.

5. While still at the breeder's, the puppies should have plenty of contact with humans; they should not vegetate somewhere off in a barn or cellar. Be suspicious if the mother dog or the puppies creep away fearfully and hide at the sight of a human.

6. Healthy puppies are frisky and alert. That applies to the mother dog as well. Therefore, watch them interact with each other and with their mother.

Note: Never buy from unscrupulous dog dealers. Even buying a puppy out of pity only lends support to such people and does them no harm. Commit to buying a puppy only after your veterinarian has examined it and found it healthy and free from serious defects, including temperament problems. Then, and only then, have you found the right dog for you.

Preventive Care for Your Dog

A strong emphasis on avoiding health problems before they start, in combination with regular veterinary visits, will be the basis of a preventive care program for your dog. Not only will you lessen the chances of debilitating injuries and diseases (and the expense of such health problems), but your dog will live a longer and healthier life.

Regular visits to the veterinarian will serve as an early warning system, not only alerting you to existing health concerns but to the possible problems you and your dog could have to face in the future. Your veterinarian will also keep your dog vaccinated against a number of canine diseases. These immunizations are usually required by law, but also constitute good preventive health care.

Your puppy will have received the first of its immunizations while still at its breeder's home. Since you have carefully chosen the source from which you purchased your puppy, made certain to get the puppy's shot record, and made the acquaintance of a good veterinarian *before* you brought the puppy home, you know what immunizations have been begun.

It Doesn't Always Have to Be a Purebred

Anyone who thinks that a mongrel—a dog resulting from various interbreedings—is the pet of his or her dreams will usually find appropriate ads in daily newspapers under the heading "Animals for Sale" or "To Give Away." Here too,

when acquiring a dog, be sure to keep in mind the points mentioned above.

With mongrels it is helpful if you know something about what breed or breeds were involved on at least one side of its lineage, so that you can make a rough estimate of the dog's size and traits.

A dog from the animal shelter: Many a future dog owner visits an animal shelter. Full-grown dogs, however, usually are not suited for novice dog owners or families with small children, especially if the dogs have already been in the shelter for some time. Often,

Jumping up and begging are habits that you should discourage.

too, information about the dog's previous life is sketchy, and therefore there is no way to guess what experiences these dogs have had in their youth. Particularly if they have grown up without an owner—or with a neglectful or abusive one—there is a danger that they lack the ability to relate well to human beings. That can make your life together difficult.

Start the Training Process Right Away

One day the time will come for the new member of your family to move into your home.

Everyone will be enthusiastic about the sweet little bundle of fur that clumsily sets about exploring its new home. At this point, most owners are not thinking a great deal about the issue of training. Moreover, many people still believe in the completely antiquated notion that a dog does not need any kind of training at all during the first 12 months.

Proper behavior in a car has to be learned as well.

On the contrary, the truth is that you have to start training the puppy—like housebreaking and basic rules of behavior—from the first day on. Every puppy, however tiny and sweet, is a real dog, and at this very moment it is in a phase of development that will mold its subsequent behavior patterns.

Its rounded appearance, described by behavioral psychologists as the little child look, triggers the parental instinct, which leads the owners to cuddle and pamper the adorable little dog baby from morning till night. Within a matter of months, however, depending on the breed, the bundle of fur will turn into a stately animal. Behavior that once evoked amused smiles from family members no longer goes over very well now. In fact certain antics can turn out to be very annoying and unpleasant in older dogs.

What the Puppy Has to Learn

The goal of all training programs is to make your dog into a pleasant, obedient companion. For the dog this also means freedom, since you can take a well-trained dog almost everywhere you go, without difficulty.

First objective: First and foremost; you have to housebreak your puppy and teach it to answer to its name.

Second objective: The puppy has to learn how it is supposed to behave in its new pack, in this case its human family. That includes knowing what it is allowed to play with and what is taboo. In playing with the pack members, it has to understand that it is not allowed to bite clothing or body parts. It should not beg at the table or help itself to food anywhere except its own dish.

Jumping up on people is another thing the dog has to unlearn early on.

In the long down *or* down-stay *position, this dog waits patiently near its owner.*

The dog's paws are not always clean, and we are not always wearing our oldest clothes. Later on, when it is fully grown, the dog—depending on the breed—sometimes can knock an adult to the ground, and it will easily knock down a child. Many dogs also jump up on cars, which often results in substantial scratches on the finish and can be dangerous, as well.

Third objective: While still a puppy, your pet has to learn to accept that it is not allowed to defend its toys or its food bowl, even when full, from humans. It has to allow everything, even the tastiest veal bone, to be taken away from it at any time. If it does not learn this, the dog will see itself as the higher-ranking member of the pack. Allowing things to be taken away has practical value as well. If the dog ever has something dangerous in its mouth—poisoned bait, or a chicken bone, for example—you can take the item away from it without difficulty.

Simple Commands

Now an overview of the first commands your dog has to learn:

Sit: This is the simplest exercise and, like all the other lessons, the *sit* command also has a practical implication.

When properly trained, your dog will learn to sit automatically when it is moving along at your side, on or off leash, and you come to a halt. In the car it will stay in the sit position until given permission to leave the vehicle. This is important in terms of its own safety. You can also teach the dog to sit automatically at the edge of every curb.

Heel: This is another exercise that teaches the basics of leash training. The dog will learn to heel, remaining at

A puppy licks the face of higher-ranking pack members—in this case, its human—as a sign of greeting or appeasement.

your left side and not pulling at the leash. Later, the dog will heel when it is off leash as well, in the *heel free.* Mastering the heel on leash and the heel free will come in handy when you are downtown with your pet, or in the park, for example.

Down: *Down* is a very important command. You can have your dog remain in the down position anywhere you choose—in front of a store or at an outdoor snack bar, for instance. Your dog should also learn to obey this command when it is some distance away from you. If it is running into a busy street because it has seen or smelled something, it can be stopped in time before a tragedy occurs. Depending on the stimulus that is acting upon the dog in such a situation, it is likely to be easier to stop the dog than to get it to turn back.

Coming when called: Naturally, your dog also has to learn to come immediately when called. It is important to start teaching this lesson while your pet is still a puppy, so that when it is fully grown it can be expected to respond in every situation.

Train Your Pet Gently— and Successfully

Proper dog training has nothing to do with drill of the parade ground type observed at some dog training sites. Our goal is to act in partnership, forming a team in which the dog happily and willingly obeys its pack leader.

A solid training in the fundamentals will allow the dog more freedom by enabling you to take your pet along and let it off leash wherever possible.

A well-trained dog, thoroughly accustomed to its environment, is unlikely to make a negative impression anywhere. On walks in the country, it will always make sure to keep in contact with its family.

Although this pet owner's manual deals only with the basics of dog training, you need to take the training program very seriously. In my courses I often have heard that the goal of many dog owners is a pet that obeys a little and comes when you call it. If you have read this far, you will understand that this is not an auspicious basis for a training program—the dog would not obey in situations in which it is really crucial to do so. Also, don't forget that basic training, or companion dog training, is the foundation for all types of more advanced training. Especially in advanced training programs that call for the dog to work largely off leash—as a hunting dog or rescue dog, for instance—or in agility training, a high level of obedience is a major prerequisite.

My tip: If you would like to provide your purebred dog with further training, join a breed club. Owners of mixed breeds, too, can join certain clubs that offer special, highly recommended activities such as agility and other similar types of dog sports. Addresses are available directly from the AKC (see Useful Addresses, page 62).

Understanding Dogs

To properly understand dogs and to have the right attitude toward them, it is helpful to make an excursion into the history of their development.

Origins of the Dog

Through various findings of research conducted by prominent behavioral scientists, it has been established that the sole progenitor of the dog is the wolf (*Canis lupus*). Other canines (*Canidae*) such as the oriental jackal (*Canis aureus*) and the coyote (*Canis latrans*) had no part in its origin. That conclusion is supported by the similarity between the brains of the wolf and the dog, in comparison with the other canines. In their facial expressions too, there are many points of correspondence between wolf and dog, although the wolf's expressions are far more differentiated. Moreover, in the wild, only the wolf and the dog mate with each other, while the dog and the oriental jackal do not, nor do the dog and the coyote.

How Wolves Live

To understand the dog, it is useful to look at the way of life of its wild ancestors, the wolves.

Life in the Pack

Wolves live in groups known as packs. Depending on the habitat and the food supply, these packs are made up of only a few animals, although they may have ten or more members. Within a pack, two hierarchies, or orders of rank, prevail: that of the females and that of the males. At the top stand an older she-wolf and an older he-wolf, respectively. They are the so-called Alpha animals. In a pack, it is usually only these two lead wolves that mate and provide offspring.

Behavior with one another: Wolves exhibit highly differentiated social behavior, which is very important for keeping the pack together.

Communication with one another: Wolves make themselves understood to one another through various means of communication, including olfactory data, visual signals, and sounds. The provision of olfactory information includes marking the territory with urine (lifting a leg). In the wolf pack, however, that behavior is reserved exclusively to the high-ranking males.

The wolf, the ancestor of all dogs, lives in packs and displays well-developed patterns of social behavior.

A lthough the dog has been the companion of humans for thousands of years, we should not forget that it is descended from the wolf and still has some characteristics of the wolf.

In this way a strange pack knows that a territory is already occupied.

Through their varied facial expressions and different body attitudes as well, wolves are able to speak with each other. When hunting for prey they develop regular hunting strategies and communicate by means of very fine nuances in their facial expressions and body attitude.

Wolves also communicate through sound. Their repertoire includes some six different basic sounds, which can be modified in intricate ways.

Aggressive disputes also occur, when there is a battle over a place in the hierarchy or when the territory has to be defended against a strange pack.

How Wolves Are Brought Up

Let's look at the way wolves are brought up.

The cubs are born in a cave. For the first ten weeks, which they spend largely in their den, they are nursed.

During the initial period the father provides food for the mother and then for the offspring as well. Later, other members of the pack assume his task.

Once the cubs are about three months old, they start to make short excursions into the surrounding area. While out, they are always accompanied by an experienced supervisor. While still cubs, they learn to adapt themselves to the pack and to respect the rules and the higher-ranking members.

In contrast to dogs, wolves can be tamed by humans only to a limited extent. Such efforts succeed only if a wolf cub has close contact with humans very soon after its birth. However, the wolf, unlike the dog, will not develop a close bond to the human. It will remain a wild animal that retains its innate aversion to humans. Dogs display this reaction only if they grow up wild and

without human contact—that is, if they fail to be influenced by humans.

Note: Erroneously, wolves continue to have a very unfortunate image in most people's minds. In contrast to dogs that are riled up, wolves will attack humans only if driven into a corner. Generally they are very cautious with strangers and prefer to flee.

How Dogs Became Domesticated

Now let's return to the wolf in our living room—the dog. Over thousands of years of domestication, the dog became a house pet. Domestication, then, is a lengthy process. During its course, animals of a species are isolated and kept and bred in human care, separated from their kin living in the wild. In captivity the process of *natural selection* (in nature, animals that are innately weaker often prematurely fall victim to stronger predatory animals) cannot occur, and it is replaced by *artificial selection*, determined exclusively by our human ideas of what is desirable. In this way, a great many different features came into being, specially cultivated by humans, depending on the dog breed.

That is the way our domestic dog came into being. It still carries its legacy from the wolf, but it is very much directed toward and dependent upon a life with human beings. Everyone who owns a dog needs to be aware of the responsibility this situation engenders.

Dogs Will Be Dogs

Although the dog has lived such a long time with humans, it has to be seen for what it is—a dog, not a human. If you anthropomorphize your pet, by viewing it as a substitute for a child or a mate, you fail to do justice to

By thoroughly investigating each other's smells, these three dogs are trying to become better acquainted.

the dog's nature. The dog's actual needs will not be met, and that can lead to behavior problems in your pet.

Training Provides a Sense of Security

Like its ancestor the wolf, the dog is a social animal and is directed toward a life in a social unit. A single wolf can scarcely survive alone, particularly if only large prey are available to it. It is dependent upon its pack. This feeling is still firmly anchored in the instincts of dogs.

For a dog, a human is its pack, and it is this fact that makes such a close relationship with a human possible.

The rigid hierarchy that prevails in a wolf pack is still in the dog's blood. The dog wants to know what position it occupies within its pack, in this case its

human family. It needs signals and rules to orient itself to some extent. They will give the dog the sense of security it needs to develop in a healthy way.

If you keep these factors in mind when dealing with your dog, it will develop a close bond with you and your family and subordinate itself cheerfully and willingly.

Only an Able Pack Leader Will Be Accepted

Understandably, a dog has to occupy the lowest-ranked spot within its human family, but the dog will willingly acknowledge the human pack leader if he or she performs convincingly in this role.

Many dog owners still are of the opinion that the best thing for their pet is to let it do whatever it wants. That

HOW-TO:
Canine Language

Dogs convey their moods largely through body language. A variety of individual signals such as the position of the ears, the attitude of the tail, and the posture of the body are combined to produce overall impressions of various kinds. If you observe your dog closely, in a short time you will know what mood it is in.

1) "I'd like to play." That is the message of the dog's play face.

Play Behavior
Drawing 1

Dogs usually place the front part of their body flat on the ground to indicate that they are extending an invitation to play. Often they bark as they do this. A dog's playful mood is often discernible from a typical expression on its face—its muzzle is slightly opened, and frequently its upper lip is drawn up slightly. The ears are always laid back, and it does not look directly at

its intended partner. These invitations then can be followed by a variety of games, including those involving racing and pulling at things.

Threatening Behavior
Drawing 2

There are two types of threatening behavior—offensive and defensive. The threat is always directed at a certain opponent (human or animal).

Offensive threat: The dog exhibits characteristic facial expressions, in addition to elements of behavior intended to impress or intimidate, such as bristling its hair and walking stiff-legged. It bares its teeth and lays its ears back (see Drawing 2). The tail points up in the air, as high as possible. In contrast to the wolf, the dog's offensive threat frequently includes biting. That invalidates the actual purpose of the threatening behavior, which is to induce the opponent to give up without a fight.

Defensive threat: The underdog makes it clear that, although it is prepared to retreat, it still is ready to attack. The ears are laid close to the back of the head, and the corners of the mouth are drawn far back, while the teeth are bared. The tail is tucked far under, pressed between the hind legs. Frequently, the dog bites. Both types of threats are accompanied by growling, barking, and yipping.

Trying to Impress or Intimidate
Drawing 3

The dog uses this behavior in an attempt to demonstrate its superiority. It tries to make itself

2) This expression indicates, "I'm about to bite."

look as large as possible, bristling the hair on its back and stretching its limbs to their full length. It stiffens its neck and carries its tail fairly high in the air. Its ears are pricked and pointed slightly forward. In this way, two males that meet each other try to determine which of them is superior. If they both feel equally strong, their efforts to impress or intimidate can turn into threatening behavior and, depending on the situation, into an actual fight.

Additional gestures are baring the teeth to bite and the so-called T sequence, in which the superior dog tries to turn its side toward the other dog (see Drawing 3).

This type of behavior also includes scratching and scraping at the ground. The dog scrapes furiously with its hind legs, usually after marking. This behavior is exhibited by very dominant dogs in particular. Mutual attempts at mounting also are part of the dog's efforts to impress.

Subservience

There are two forms of this behavioral pattern—active and passive submission.

Active submission, also known as social greeting, involves a display of friendliness by a lower-ranking dog to a higher-ranking one. The lower-ranking dog, seeking muzzle contact with the higher-ranking one, seems to be crouching down. Its tail wags fairly rapidly but is held rather low. The corners of the dog's mouth are pulled back and its ears are laid back.

If a dog behaves this way toward a human, it is trying to lick the hands and face. This behavior, which originates in puppyhood, is a way of persuading the parents to cough out food.

Giving a paw is a gesture of submissiveness or appeasement. It has its origin in the puppy's effort to obtain nourishment. While suckling, puppies push against the mother dog's teats to express milk. Dogs also give their paw when begging for food or attention (see photo, inside front cover).

Passive submission is exhibited by a dog when it throws itself to the ground in a fight, for example. It lies down on its back to demonstrate that it is the underdog, and clasps its tail firmly between its legs. Its ears are laid all the way back on the head and it avoids eye contact with the opponent. This behavior induces the higher-ranking dog to break off the fight.

The Relaxed Dog

Depending on the breed, the dog's tail will hang down, slightly bent. The ears are pricked and pointed forward. The legs are bent at a slight angle and the head is slightly raised.

The Uncertain Dog

The dog seems to cower slightly. Its glance is restless. Its ears are turned toward the back, and its tail is clasped between its legs. Usually, the corners of its mouth are drawn back.

Olfactory Communication

Dogs obtain olfactory information about other members of their species by mutual sniffing at the tail area and hindquarters as well as the droppings. A dog can also acquire information from human smells.

The Dog's Vocalizations

Barking: To a greater degree than wolves, dogs use barking as a means of communication. It can vary widely, depending on the breed and the bark's intended meaning.

Howling: Many dogs howl for many different reasons, for example, when a church bell rings or when they feel lonely.

Growling: This is a threatening noise, directed at an opponent. You should always approach a growling dog with caution. Growling is also used as a warning noise when the dog sees or hears something unfamiliar.

Whimpering, yowling, and yipping: These sounds express uneasiness, fear, or pain.

3) "I'm stronger than you" is the message the long-haired dog is trying to convey to the other dog. Planting itself in front of its opponent by displaying its broad side, this dog is making an effort to intimidate.

This attitude shows total relaxation.

does not give the dog the feeling of living in an intact pack, however, because it lacks a clearly drawn line. If such a dog has a very strong personality, it will one day try to become pack leader itself, so that its pack is capable of surviving.

Also completely outmoded is the opinion that during a dog's first year of life it should be granted great latitude of action, with serious training beginning only after that first year. As you now know, wolf cubs, while they are still young, have to become integrated into the pack and accept certain rules. The same is true of dogs.

Because of their social nature, dogs prefer to be constantly with their family members. Nevertheless, an adult dog should not be upset by having to spend a few hours alone from time to time.

It is not right, however, to leave a dog by itself all day, whether inside your house or outside in its kennel. That usually results in behavior problems; because being alone runs completely contrary to the dog's nature.

The Language of Dogs

To properly understand dogs, you have to know how they communicate with us and with other members of their species. Like the wolf, they do so by means of visual, auditory, and olfactory signals (see HOW-TO, pages 14 and 15).

Visual signals make up a large part of the range of communication. Moods are signaled through facial expressions, ear position, tail attitude, and the hair on the back. Unfortunately, many breeds have lost some of these means of communication as a result of selective breeding. For example, most greyhounds always carry their tail between their legs and thus they appear submissive at all times, even when they are not. The beagle, however, is always in an attitude of striving to impress, by virtue of its upright tail. Breeds like the boxer and the spaniel no longer can convey much at all due to their docked tails.

In the transmission of visual signals, the ears play a major role. Here, breeds with drooping ears are similarly limited in their capacity for expression. Many breeds are at a disadvantage when it comes to bristling their hair as well. The poodle and the Old English sheepdog, for example, are denied that means of expression. Such dogs sometimes can have problems communicating with others of their species. For this reason it is very important that a dog have plenty of contact with other dogs while it is a puppy, so that it can learn social behavior.

Your dog also has the ability to tell from your facial expressions, the loudness of your voice, your movements, and your tone how you feel toward it. This is an innate ability. In addition, during its development when young, the dog learns to interpret certain combinations of the signals listed above and the actions that follow them. It can recognize very fine nuances that often completely elude us humans. For instance, all the members of the family are sitting together. The pack leader leaves the room once or twice to get something. When he goes out of the room for the third time, he is planning to get ready for a walk with the dog. The dog, which had been lying quietly under the table, now stands expectantly in front of its master and wags its tail, although he has said nothing at all about a walk. Minute differences in posture and facial expression, however, let the dog know that now it is to be included.

Olfactory signals: It is well known that dogs obtain information about others of their species by mutual sniffing. It is also certain that a dog can derive various kinds of information from the different scents that a human gives off when feeling stress or anxiety, for example. Since a human cannot even come close to sensing the same thing as the dog, we do not know exactly what role smells play in communication between humans and dogs.

Auditory signals: Dogs communicate with each other and with humans by means of varied sounds such as barking or growling.

How Dogs Learn

Dogs are very capable of learning and adapting. In contrast to wild animals, they are capable of mastering learning processes that go beyond vital necessities such as the search for food. Indeed, one can even say that they are capable of simple discerning action.

Everyone knows that a dog can be taught a great variety of commands and behaviors. But how does the dog learn them?

Digging is one of dogs' passions.

Basically, dogs learn through experience. Modes of behavior that are connected with positive experiences are repeated eagerly, while those linked with negative experiences tend to be avoided.

Dogs are capable of different processes of learning:

Classical conditioning: Here a certain stimulus triggers a reflex; for example, a dog likes to lick out empty yogurt containers. When you eat yogurt, the spoon makes a certain sound on the bottom of the container when it is almost empty. Then the dog is allowed to lick the container clean. After some time the sound alone is enough to make the dog's mouth water.

Conditioned aversion: Another learning process is conditioned aversion; for example, a dog steals cake from the table. If it is scolded with a loud *"No!,"* it will avoid this situation in the future. A certain stimulus, then, is followed by a bad experience. (Never use violence—or even the threat of it—to mold a dog's behavior. Animals so conditioned can develop vicious tendencies, or else they may become timid, cowering at their owner's every move. So put away those rolled-up newspapers and those menacing straps! The idea of wielding such props to intimidate your dog—even if you have no intention of actually using them—is without merit.)

Operant conditioning: Some dog owners demand, often unconsciously, a certain behavior; for example, a dog is limping because it is injured. Its mistress feels very sorry for it and bestows special attention upon it. When it has recovered, it continues to limp, in order to get this attention again.

This type of process is called operant learning or operant conditioning.

Conditioned inhibition: In the learning of a conditioned inhibition, an undesirable behavior such as cat-chasing, is prevented before it begins. In this case, a threatening *no* when a cat comes into view, stops the dog before it chases the cat, not when it comes back home after the fact. With appropriate watchfulness on your part, this presents no great difficulty. All you have to do is to discover the cat before the dog has seen it and begins to chase it.

Conditioned appetence: Last, we come to the learning of conditioned appetitive behavior. Here the dog learns to combine a certain stimulus or a certain action with a certain course of behavior; for example, a dog that loves the water goes into raptures when its mistress picks up the special ring it uses as a water toy because it knows it is going to go for a swim.

The Most Common Misunderstandings between Dog and Human

Because of domestication (see page 12) a dog is more likely to associate with a human than with other dogs, but within its human family it lives as it would in a pack of dogs. A dog does not see a human as a member of its own species in the true sense, of course. It is well able to distinguish between a human and a dog, yet it considers a human a kind of super-dog. That means that a dog in a certain sense expects doglike behavior of a human.

Conversely, however, humans frequently see a dog as a kind of human and often measure it by their own standards. This fundamental misunderstanding gives rise to most of the other common misunderstandings between dog and human in their daily interactions.

First misunderstanding: Many dog owners think they are inhibiting their dog when they train it and work with it, but the opposite is true.

In the wild, wolves or wild dogs are constantly challenged. They have to kill prey and develop hunting strategies for that purpose. They fight over the individual positions in the order of rank, and their territory has to be defended against interlopers. By domesticating the dog, we have relieved it of all these responsibilities. Therefore, to keep our pet from becoming mentally dull and unstimulated, we have to provide it with appropriate activity.

Second misunderstanding: Humans often use human standards to measure a dog in the sphere of its emotional life.

Dogs lack a true understanding of human feelings. If you are in a good mood and relaxed, the positive feelings you radiate are communicated to your pet. If you are sad or irritated, that saddens the dog. It is disconcerted by the altered behavior of its owner but it does not know what is actually going on inside the person.

A dog also lacks a conscience in the human sense. For the dog, there is no distinction between good and evil. What often appears to be a guilty conscience in a dog is not only fear of punishment, but, even more, an innate pattern of mimetic signs indicating submissiveness and appeasement. Through this behavior the dog seeks permission to remain in the pack even though it has violated existing rules.

Third misunderstanding: There are dog owners who believe that their pet is well accommodated in an outdoor kennel or run, and that it is sufficient to bring the dog out of the kennel to the training site from time to time, work with it there, and put it away again afterwards. Kept in such isolation and possibly even made aggressive toward humans by amateurish training, such dogs often represent a serious threat.

All too frequently, owners anthropomorphize—ascribe human characteristics to—their dogs. That hardly does justice to a dog's needs, however. Dealing appropriately with a dog is crucial to its healthy development.

The Developmental Phases of Puppies

This important chapter will help you gain an even better understanding of your pet and treat it appropriately.

Critical Phases of Development

A puppy's development occurs in various phases. The rest of its life will be influenced by the experiences it has—or fails to have—during these formative periods. Therefore, it is important to make the fullest use of these phases.

During its first year of life a dog passes through decisive periods of development.

In each of these phases its brain is receptive to certain specific stimuli and experiences. Experiences during these phases leave their imprint on the dog; in other words, they are fixed almost indelibly in its brain.

Absence of these stimuli during the phase intended for their reception will result in a developmental deficiency. These deficiencies are very difficult, often impossible, to compensate for later on. Most behavioral peculiarities in adult dogs were caused by shortcomings in puppyhood.

The First Eight Weeks of Life

A puppy is still blind at birth; however, it manages to find, by its own efforts, the thing that is of the greatest importance to it at the moment—its mother's teat. There it can satisfy its need to suck and its hunger. That is its first educational achievement.

At the age of about two to three weeks, the puppy's eyes open and it can consciously perceive its mother and littermates, that is, it becomes acquainted with other members of its species. Now the first critical phase of development—the imprinting phase—begins. During this stage the puppy learns its first lessons in social behavior from its mother and littermates. For this reason it is crucial that the mother dog be in good health and behave normally.

The imprinting phase lasts until approximately the eighth week.

Keep in mind: The puppy's imprinting phase begins in about the third week of life. This is the time when bonding to humans should also occur. That means that puppies need intense contact, including a great deal of physical handling, with humans, so that they view them, in a way, as fellow members of their species and thus become able to live together with them in harmony.

When the puppies make their first excursions into the area surrounding their whelping box, they should have an opportunity to receive a great many stimuli. Good breeders will arrange a kind of play area for their puppies and acquaint them with a variety of visual and auditory stimuli. In brief, they will enable the pups to become acquainted with their environment.

Weeks 8 to 12

The socialization phase, which lasts until about the twelfth week, begins in approximately the eighth week.

Although until now it was the mother alone who took care of her puppies, among dogs living in the wild the father and other pack members as well make an appearance at this time, to begin training the puppies.

With their mother's help, these collie pups are exploring their surroundings.

Until this point the puppies had enjoyed great latitude of action. Everyone looked after them, and the adult dogs tolerated everything. Now that will change. Starting right now, the puppies will be reprimanded by growls or a vigorous shake of their nape when they go too far in their antics. There will continue to be frequent playtimes, however, with the adult dog deciding when and how long the puppies can play and thus emphasizing its dominant position.

In this way the puppies learn to respect the authority of the adult dogs and the rules that apply in the pack.

Keep in mind: When a puppy joins your household at the age of roughly eight weeks, it has been accustomed to having everything revolve around it. It was allowed to do as it wished, was nursed when it was hungry, and so forth.

Now it considers you and your family its new pack. To a certain extent it will now test you to see how far it can go and what it can do with the objects in its new home.

Now it becomes clear, if it wasn't already, how important it is to start training the puppy the very first day and to familiarize it with the rules that apply in its new family. To accomplish that, you need to establish some taboos for the puppy.

It has to understand that many things, such as chair legs, rugs, and the like, are no-nos.

Playing together now ranks high in importance. In the first eight weeks the puppy plays almost exclusively on its own with an object of some kind, or with individual parts of its littermates' bodies. Now it begins to recognize that it is much more fun to do something jointly. And joint activity promotes bonding between owner and dog. Playing has another purpose as well, however. If the puppy gets too wild during the game, you should simply end the play period abruptly. That will have an inhibitory effect on the puppy's impulse to bite a human being.

By playing together and learning that some things it would like to do are not allowed, the puppy learns that it is advantageous to live together and to adapt itself to a community.

It is also very important to give the puppy plenty of opportunity to play with nonviolent dogs of all ages, though principally of approximately its same age, so that it learns social behavior among its peers. For this purpose, breed clubs and other associations offer imprinting play days, which I recommend attending (see Useful Addresses, page 62).

Shortcomings in the socialization phase, such as lack of firmness and disagreement within the family over what the dog may and may not do, can lead to serious problems with the dog later on.

Weeks 12 to 20

Within the next two months your puppy will become a young dog. In a pack of dogs, an order of rank gradually develops at this time, however with the emphasis more on mental than on physical superiority. The father dog becomes more and more a role model and makes an impression on his

In the first few weeks of a puppy's life, its mother plays the most important role. She gives it nourishment, provides it with a sense of security, and plays with it.

puppies largely through his experience and his demeanor, rather than his physical superiority. Therefore, the puppies feel quite secure under their father's wing and gladly subordinate themselves to him. The excursions they make into a nearby area now and the hunting trips they make later give them knowledge of their environment and allow them to gain valuable experience.

Keep in mind: This phase of development is taxing for the dog owner. Lacking littermates, the puppy now will test yóu to see who has the upper hand. It wants to know precisely how it stands with its pack leader, the alpha dog, and whether that leader is also suited to lead the pack.

Some young dogs begin to defend their food bowl by growling. It would be misguided, however, to respect that and allow the dog to eat undisturbed, because that tells the dog that it has the upper hand and possibly reinforces it in further efforts to become pack leader—rightly so, from its point of view, since the current alpha dog obviously lacks the appropriate qualities, and that means the pack is in danger. In such a situation, take the food bowl away from your pet, and do not give it back until the dog's behavior is friendly again.

Remain firm. Violating previously accepted prohibitions also is characteristic of this phase of development. It is especially important now to remain firm and consistent so these problems will quickly subside. Moreover, the young dog will be certain that it has a good pack leader in whose care it can feel safe and secure and upon whose guidance it can rely. This results in a relationship of trust and a strong bond between dog and owner. Both are essential for a harmonious life together.

Off leash. On its daily short walks, the puppy should be off leash whenever possible to explore its surroundings on its own. This will help to strengthen the bond between you, because the puppy will automatically keep looking in your direction to make sure it does not lose sight of the thing most important for its survival—its pack.

Playing with other dogs its own age helps a puppy learn social behavior within its species.

You can further reinforce that with a little game. At a moment when the puppy's attention is distracted, hide behind a bush or something similar—not too far away, of course. After a short time, your little dog will notice that you are not there and start to look for you. Once it finds you, of course, you need to make a great show of your delight.

As soon as your dog knows its name, it is quite important to call it only once—twice at most—when you are outdoors. If it fails to react, you should take off in the opposite direction at a lively pace. This is the only way the puppy will learn a lifelong lesson—to come immediately when it is called. If you run after your pet, it will interpret your action as an invitation to play. However, if you wait for the dog and keep calling it, that will tell it that it doesn't need to hurry, since everyone is still there.

Unfortunately, there are many dog owners who always keep their puppy on leash or even carry the dog, out of fear that it could run away or that something could happen to it. In this way they repress investigative behavior, prevent important contacts with other dogs, and put a stop to the development of an excellent relationship. The result is a dog that tends to react fearfully to its surroundings and to other members of its species. Some dogs also become aggressive, since they feel especially powerful in your arms or on leash. It is quite possible that such a dog, if it inadvertently is off leash, will run away to compensate for those things that have been denied to it so far in its life.

Working dog. If you want to use your pet as a working dog—for hunting, for instance—now is the best time to prepare it for its future duties. For a

After playing, it's time to take a break.

hunting dog, that would mean becoming familiar with rabbit skins and bird feathers, and getting used to the water.

General tips: During this phase of development it is important to get the dog increasingly used to its environment and to familiarize it with a variety of situations. It must get used to sources of noise of all sorts and descriptions, such as lawn mowers, mixers, vacuum cleaners, traffic noise, and so forth. You'll have to practice walking with it on stairs and floors of all types, as well as over narrow footpaths, through tight passageways, and over bridges. Confront your dog with all kinds of situations, such as large groups of people or fluttering pieces of paper.

For the first excursion downtown, incidentally, you need to take extra time and not plan it as part of your regular shopping trip. All of this helps the dog learn to find its way around in our civilized, high-tech surroundings, and to keep it from exhibiting anxiety in everyday situations.

From the Sixth Month On

By the age of roughly six months, your dog already has passed through the phases that will be decisive for the remaining years of its life. If you take the utmost advantage of those phases, then you will have a faithful companion who places you, its owner, at the center of its life. It will willingly and happily subordinate itself to you.

Now the dog can readily distinguish between work and play, and its further training will not entail any significant problems. Your dog will try not to lose sight of you, and will not go out of your range of vision or hearing without your permission.

Behavioral researcher Konrad Lorenz used the term *loyalty* for this behavior.

Encounters with adult dogs are also important for a puppy.

Becoming Adult

Depending on your pet's breed, it will take six to 12 months more for the dog to become fully grown. During this time, puberty will occur. It may be that your pet once again questions some rule or another. It may also be that in some situations it temporarily reacts somewhat sensitively or fearfully. If you persevere and remain firm and consistent, this time too will pass without problems, thanks to the good relationship and trust that exist between you and your dog.

HOW-TO:
Getting Settled

Making Preparations

Even before the puppy comes through the door of its new home, everything should be in readiness for it. It needs bowls for food and water, a collar, and a leash (lead). A bed also has to be made ready. Upon arrival, the little dog should find a few toys waiting for it.

1) Wicker baskets are pretty, but make sure the one you purchase is strong enough to withstand a puppy's chewing.

Don't forget the dog food. Ask the breeder what he or she has been feeding the puppy. During the initial period, it is best to use the same food as the breeder, to avoid forcing the puppy to make a sudden switch of diet. Changes in its feeding plan should always be made gradually. Some breeders will give you enough food for the first few days at home.

The Dog's Bed
Drawing 1

Baskets made of wicker, plastic sleeping boxes, and cavelike pet homes made of washable materials are available in pet stores. The cavelike quarters are more suitable for the small dog breeds.

Since a puppy is frightened by suddenly being separated from its mother and littermates, it is best to set up its bed in or near your bedroom. Then you will also notice right away if the puppy has to relieve itself during the night. Don't play with your new pet at night; it might become accustomed to it.

My tip: To make it easier for the puppy to feel at home, especially at night, try this useful trick: Arrange for the breeder to put a towel, for example, in with the puppies. When you pick up your new pet, take the towel along and lay it in the dog's little basket at home. In this way, it will still have near it the familiar smell of its mother and littermates.

Dog Toys
Drawing 2

Pet stores offer a large selection of toys. There are many types available, ranging from squeaking rubber cutlets to rings and balls for throwing, and knotted rope aids for retrieve training. If, from the beginning, you give your pet nothing but toys designed specifically for dogs, it will not be so easily tempted to use shoes or household items as playthings.

Transportation

The time has come for your new family member to be brought home from the breeder's. Frequently, the breeder does not live close by, and the puppy has a fairly long trip to make. If you go by car to pick it up, you should take a companion along, so that one of you can look after the little puppy during the trip. Before traveling to its new home—whether by plane, train, or car—the puppy should not be given food, so that it does not get sick en route. That could ruin the idea of traveling for your pet for some time to come!

When going back home by car, take hourly breaks to let the puppy get a little exercise and to relieve itself. It is essential to

2) Toys for your pet are a must. Pet stores sell a large assortment, ranging from chew rings to pull toys made of plastic.

3) When you carry the puppy, hold it firmly around the chest and support the hindquarters.

Dealing with the puppy: Of its own accord, the puppy may seek to make contact with everyone. Show it its toys and bed. If you want to pick up the pup, Drawing 3 will show you the proper way to hold it.

If the little dog starts to chew on rugs or chair legs on its very first round of the house, don't hesitate to make it clear from the beginning that such activities are not allowed.

Sleeping: If the puppy had a lengthy, tiring trip to your home, it might like to take a nap before long (see Drawing 4). If that is the case, let it have its rest. That

tant in establishing hierarchical relationships and teaching the puppy not to bite. If the dog gets too wild in its play, call a halt to the game. That is fairly easy for an adult; however, if the dog is playing with a child, which may not be much bigger than it is, that could be much more difficult. Children are not yet able to tell when the puppy has to be reprimanded; therefore, you should never let children play alone with the young dog, and be sure to end the game if the puppy gets too excited.

Going for a walk: Don't overtax the puppy on walks. During

keep the puppy on leash at these times.

If both you and the breeder happen to live near an airport, it is best to transport the dog by plane. Contact the airline ahead of time.

Transport the puppy by train only if you are picking it up yourself; otherwise, it would be left alone too long.

Arrival
Drawings 3 and 4

It is a great turning point in the puppy's life when it leaves its mother and littermates and goes to new surroundings. You need to respect that and let the little dog explore its new home in peace and quiet.

4) A puppy needs a lot of sleep. It should not be disturbed during its rest time.

applies in the future as well—a sleeping puppy should *never* be disturbed.

Games and Walks

Playing: During its waking phases, your new pet will be ready for all kinds of games. Playing together is very impor-

the first few weeks, one or two ten-minute walks per day are enough. This amount should be increased slowly. Continue to expose your pet to unfamiliar environments on exploratory walks, so that it can gain new experiences and impressions.

Basic Course for Trainers

The most important things in training a dog are consistency and firmness. That is the only way the dog can learn what place it holds in the family and what rules apply to it. Also, your pet will acquire a feeling of security and trust.

To make the training of your dog a success, it is important to observe certain rules right from the beginning. These rules will make learning easier for the dog and help it recognize what its assigned place in the family is to be. Some training, like housebreaking and basic rules of behavior, should begin as soon as your puppy comes into your home. Other serious training for your puppy probably shouldn't start much before six months of age. Of course, some dogs will be ready for training earlier than others. Your dog's level of physical and mental maturity will dictate its readiness for training. The veterinarian will help you decide when your pup is old enough for lessons to be meaningful.

If you have never trained a dog, you would be well-advised to seek help from an experienced trainer. Training should be an enjoyable experience, and someone who thoroughly knows the breed will be able to help you keep things both enjoyable and productive.

In this chapter I have put together a list of the most important training rules for you.

Be Consistent

Consistency is one of the most critical rules of dog training. It is essential for all family members to be in agreement about what the dog is and is not allowed to do. D not let one member of the family allow the dog to sit on the couch, for example, while another does not. Moreover, the couch and the bed are, from the dog's point of view, elevated places to rest, and, in packs of dogs or wolves, such places are reserved exclusively for high-ranking animals. Thus, it is better not to give your dog a chance to get comfortable on the sofa or bed.

Only One Trainer

While your pet is being trained, your family needs to designate one adult member to practice regularly with the dog. That will make it easier for the dog to learn the commands. Later on, other household members should agree to use the same commands, to avoid confusing the dog.

Your Voice Is Crucial

The dog takes its cues to a great extent from the inflection of the human voice and the sound of individual words. It does not, however, have a real understanding of the words.

Commands should always be given in a firm, decisive tone of voice at normal volume. It is unnecessary, as well as inadvisable, to shout at the dog.

Praise and Scolding

Praise: If your dog has obeyed a command nicely, don't forget to praise it. Use a higher register for words of praise.

It is important to praise the dog in such a way that it can tell you are glad. With some dogs it is enough to pet them a little; with others, effusive praise is necessary. For emphasis you can also give your pet an edible reward from time to time, but don't make a habit of it. You certainly don't want your dog to obey only when it is hungry.

By practicing in a group, a dog learns not to be distracted by other dogs.

Scolding: There are situations in which you have to discipline your pet. That is nothing unnatural for the dog, since in a canine pack it would also be reprimanded if it had violated the rules. However, it is important that the dog also understand what you want to convey to it and why it is being reprimanded.

With many dogs, a loud, sharp *"No!"* is sufficient. There are many thick-skinned dogs for which that is not enough, however. In such a case, in addition to the *no,* you can place one hand on each side of the dog's face and look at it sternly. If that isn't adequate either, take hold of its coat firmly at the nape and give the dog a shake (see photo, back cover). The next step, if one is necessary, is to lift it up by the coat on the nape, so that only the hind legs are still on the ground. With some dogs, even that does not work. In these cases, grasp the dog—if you are strong enough—by the nape and the rump, and lift it off the ground. Another possibility would be to lay it on its back and hold it firmly by the throat until it will stay in that position of its own accord.

Some punishments are incomprehensible to the dog, such as making it go without a meal or locking it in the basement. Often we unconsciously praise or scold in such a way as to achieve the exact opposite of what we really intended. That is the case, for example, when the dog barks or growls at someone for no reason and we then pet it and talk soothingly to it. The dog will interpret our behavior as approval.

Note: Both praise and scolding have to follow the given behavior immediately. A dog always connects praise and discipline with the behavior it exhibited most recently. A typical error—one commonly made—is to punish the dog

29

when it finally comes back to you after you have called it repeatedly or after undertaking a scouting trip without your permission. Since the dog in this case connects the punishment with its return, you are achieving the precise opposite of what you really intend.

Give Clear Commands

Commands have to be brief and clear, since a dog cannot grasp the meaning of an entire sentence. Give only the actual command, together with the dog's name; for example, say *"Toby, heel,"* not *"Come on, be a good dog and heel."*

If the dog has mixed up two commands, you need to correct it. That takes some practice as well. Here's an example: You give your pet the *down* command, but the dog sits instead. The right move now is to go to the dog, repeat the command, and guide it into the *down* position. That way it will understand what you want of it. But, if you go up to it and explain, *You're supposed to do down now, not sit,* you'll only confuse it. It will hear two commands and not know what it is supposed to do next. And that brings us to the next point.

Require Commands to Be Obeyed at Once

If your dog is to develop a good level of obedience, it has to know that it needs to obey a command without delay. Make sure that your pet carries out an order the first time, as soon as it has understood it. If you have to repeat the command, do so while applying a little correction as well. The more often you repeat the same command without insisting that the dog carry it out, the more watered down the notion will become and the less your pet can be counted on to obey.

Commands Should Be Carried Out to the Letter

Make sure your dog always carries out an exercise exactly. You are not doing your pet a favor if one day you generously let it get by with sloppy work and then punish it for the same kind of work the next day. The dog will be unable to get its bearings, and will get rattled.

Finish the Exercises Correctly

If you have given the dog a command, it is very important that you also terminate it in some way, whether by starting another exercise or by ending the practice session; for example, if you have ordered the dog to lie down somewhere in your home, don't forget about it—you have to come back and release it.

Practice Takes Time

Allow plenty of time for drill sessions. Always begin a session with an exercise that the dog has already learned. The session should always be ended by the dog handler, not by the dog, which may feel disinclined to continue. If you see that your pupil would prefer to play, have it do two more exercises correctly and then give it its freedom. Always conclude a lesson with an exercise that the dog already knows, to let it feel successful. That is especially necessary if previously you were teaching a new command that did not work.

Don't introduce a new exercise until the dog has mastered all the previous commands. Incidentally, it is not advisable to have the dog repeat a command too many times in succession. That spoils its enjoyment of the training program. If an exercise goes well, repeat it once or twice, then start a new one.

The Right Equipment

For your dog's training program, you need the following equipment:

For a puppy:
- Leather or cloth collar
- Leather or cloth leash (lead)

The collar and the leash should be in keeping with the size of the dog and not too heavy.

The collar should not exert any pull or tension, since that is not necessary with a puppy and might even be harmful.

My tip: If you also want to train your pet to respond to whistle signals—which I highly recommend—you should buy your puppy, for future use, a special whistle used for training hunting dogs. It can be used for all dogs (see page 32).

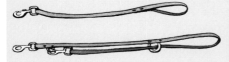

For an adult dog:
- Collar with limited or unlimited tension effect, made of metal, leather, or cloth.

- Leash with a mechanism for adjusting its length. It can be made of leather or cloth (see Putting on the Collar and Leash Properly, drawing, page 43).

My tip: Metal leashes and leashes that retract automatically are not suitable for training a dog.

Note: With very strong, hard-headed dogs you can temporarily use a so-called training collar, also known as a spiked collar. Here it is important to attach the snap hook of the leash to both metal rings of the collar. In this way, without harming your pet, you can effectively imitate the grasp on the nape that mother dogs use to train their puppies. The rounded spikes, which point inward, will not injure the dog, but will exert pressure all the way around when you tug on the leash—without choking the dog.

The length of this leash is adjustable. It is suitable for training an adult dog.

Dog Training Programs in Action

Two Levels of Training

In the preceding chapters you learned why training your dog is important, how you can gain a better understanding of your pet, and what you have to keep in mind when training it. Now I would like to explain to you, step by step, the proper way to teach each individual exercise to your dog.

As I have stated, you should start the training program while your dog is still a puppy. At this stage its willingness to learn and capacity for learning are at their most pronounced.

An adult dog, also, is still capable of being trained, although it can no longer learn to obey as easily as a dog that is accustomed to do so from the very outset.

Since the exercises for puppies and those for adolescent dogs differ in their degree of difficulty, the following portion of this manual is divided into two parts:
• Training a Puppy, and
• Training a Companion Dog.

Teaching Exercises Properly

The training should be spread over the course of the day. Some exercises can be taught indoors, others in the yard or during a walk. New exercises always should be practiced with the dog on leash and without any distractions—preferably in your own home or yard.

Once the dog has comprehended a command, gradually increase the amount of distraction. Now you can also drill the dog in the park, first on leash and later off leash.

Make sure that you give a command only when you are certain that you can correct the dog immediately, if necessary.

Example: Don't shout "Sit" at your young dog when it is involved in playing with other dogs. In this situation, it is too distracted and will almost certainly not obey. Then the dog would learn that it doesn't matter whether it obeys or not.

"Multilingual" Training for Dogs

You can teach the individual commands to your pet in different languages. That means your dog will learn to perform certain exercises in response to verbal commands, auditory signals given with a whistle (see reference to whistles for training hunting dogs, page 31), and hand signals.

Hand signals and whistle signals are very practical and effective, since a blow of the whistle, for example, often is more successful than a spoken command. In addition, the different languages often add greater variety to the training sessions.

In the following two chapters I will indicate at the beginning of each exercise whether hand signals and whistle signals are applicable, and explain how to give either type of signal correctly.

The most effective obedience training begins with the puppy training program and gradually merges into companion dog training. As a rule, you should practice with your dog only when you are not under any time constraint.

Having your dog run next to a bicycle takes diligent practice (see Your Dog as a Recreational Partner, page 51).

Training a Puppy

A puppy must be trained with lots of patience and without force. Alternate short training periods with lengthy play breaks for the puppy. And remember: be firm and consistent during the practice session.

The best method of training a puppy is positive conditioning. That means you create situations in which the dog does, of its own accord, what you want it to do. You work with the dog without direct force and with a great deal of patience (see How Dogs Learn, page 17).

In work with a puppy, play should predominate. Drill for approximately one to two minutes, then follow up with an extensive break for play.

Practice with the puppy before it is fed, and do not practice when it is about to have a nap.

It is important to hold regular training sessions with your pet. With a puppy, two to four minutes of training two to three times a day will be enough. Always remember that your dog, regardless of its good qualities, is still just a dog. Your puppy will want to learn the lessons you want to teach it. Be patient with this young dog. Always adapt your training to the speed of the dog's learning.

The Puppy Learns Its Name

The first thing your puppy has to learn is to answer to its name. If its breeder has already gotten it used to the name, the puppy will know its name when it joins your household. If not, always say its name in connection with something positive—when you pet it, for example, or when you feed it. In this way, it will learn to respond to its name.

Housebreaking

The next learning objective is housebreaking your pet.

Basically, a puppy usually has to relieve itself after every meal, every time it wakes up, and while it is playing. Keep a close eye on the puppy, and take it outside as soon as you notice that
- it is walking around sniffing at the floor, or
- turning around in a circle while it looks for a likely spot.

Once it has relieved itself outdoors, shower it with praise.

If you consistently observe the puppy and always manage to get it outside in time, your little dog will be housebroken within about two weeks.

Never rub the puppy's nose in excrement or urine. The puppy won't understand what you're doing, and in addition, you'll have to wash it. Furthermore, you should *never* strike a puppy, for any reason, but certainly not for messing in your house. Swatting a puppy will do nothing but make the youngster fear and resent you. Shouting at a puppy is also futile. You can break the puppy's concentration by clapping your hands and you can let it know it isn't doing the right thing by saying *"No"* in a firm, authoritarian (alpha male) voice.

My tip: Make it a habit to say the same thing—*"Hurry up,"* for example— every time the dog defecates. Then you can succeed in getting the dog to do its business almost on command.

Note: If your pet does have an accident in your home, don't punish it. Remove all traces of the mishap as described above.

In addition to planned feeding times and regular relief outings, you can help your puppy through housebreaking in several other ways:

• Always emphasize with praise the times your pup does what it should, where it should.

• Feed a high-quality puppy food with good digestibility. The stool from this type of food will be smaller and firmer, an added benefit if an inside mistake does occur, and much easier for a young dog to hold than a loose, runny stool.

• Never feed table scraps. Not only are they nutritionally unbalancing but they may actually bring on diarrhea and/or vomiting.

• Do not leave food out for your pup all day long; your youngsters will actually do better on three to four small meals a day.

• Never put food items (biscuits, edible treats, etc.) in the dog's house or on its pillow. The puppy will not be able to keep its den area clean if bits of food are always present.

• Discourage messes by thoroughly cleaning up any that do occur. Deodorize an accident spot on the floor to prevent your puppy from catching its scent and repeating the act.

Introduction to the Collar and Leash

The first commands should be practiced with the dog on leash at all times. Then you can administer a correction at any time, and it will be impressed upon the puppy early on that it has no other option but to obey.

Getting the dog used to the leash and collar: For many dogs this presents no difficulty, and they soon accept both collar and leash.

It is helpful if you get the puppy used to the collar first. At the beginning, put the collar on your pet in your home, for a few hours at a time. Once it accepts the collar, attach the leash as well. First, it probably will resist this curb on its freedom by straining at the leash. Then try strolling around a bit with the dog on leash. Or, let the dog lead you around at first.

Leash Training

As soon as the puppy accepts the leash and collar, teach it to stay at your left side at all times (see photo, page 36).

Heel

How to practice: Take the leash in your right hand. For correction, use both hands. Use your left hand to indicate praise.

The puppy's head should be about level with its owner's knee. That is the only way it can get the message in time when you are changing direction or

The positive stimulus of the dog biscuit induces the puppy to assume the down position. Reinforce this by stroking the dog's back (see Lying Down, page 38).

The puppy is being trained by means of positive stimuli, such as food. This is a way of getting the pup to do of its own accord what you expect of it.

Teaching the dog to heel on leash.

The puppy is learning the sit position.

speed later on. That means that the dog's head should be neither ahead of (forging) nor behind (lagging) the trainer's leg. A treat in your left hand will motivate the dog to stay at your left side. Give the *heel* command and start walking. If the dog hesitates and stops, coax it to move forward. If it moves ahead quickly, falls behind, or pulls firmly to the side, correct it with a swift, sharp tug on the leash, so that it ends up at your left side again, and repeat the *heel* command, praising the dog when it lines up with you again. Then you should pet it and praise it immediately, while continuing to move ahead and letting the leash hang loosely again. In this way, the puppy will learn that being at its owner's left side is always an agreeable experience.

The sharp tug on the leash is extremely important. If you pull the dog along slowly, it will offer increasing resistance. Then your training will produce a dog that constantly strains at its leash, which will be unpleasant later on, especially with big dogs.

At first, walk only short distances with the puppy, and always move straight ahead. Once that is working well, incorporate curves in your path of movement, first gradual ones and then sharper ones.

Don't forget to keep taking breaks for play, so that the puppy is not overtaxed.

Sitting

One of the easiest exercises is the *sit*.
• Command: *sit*.

- Hand signal: Raised right forefinger.

How to practice: This exercise should be drilled only on leash at first. Hold the leash in your left hand. In your right hand, hold either a little treat or a full bowl of dog food. The puppy should be either at your left side or in front of you.

Now give the *sit* command. Hold the treat or the food bowl so that the puppy has to look up at it. Wait until the dog sits down of its own accord. In that position, it will be able to look upward more comfortably.

When the dog is sitting, wait a moment before giving it its food. In addition, of course, you should reward it with lavish praise and petting. It is helpful to praise the dog for sitting by scratching its chest. That will encourage it to remain in the sit position. If you stroke its back, the puppy might be inclined to lie down.

Once the puppy has grasped the *sit* command, give it a treat only from time to time. After all, you most assuredly do not want a dog that obeys only when it is hungry.

If this method of teaching your dog to sit by means of edible incentives does not work, there is another way. Squat down at your dog's right side and, with your right hand, keep the leash quite short. Then, as you give the command, use your left hand to press the puppy's rump gently but firmly downward. With this method too, remember to praise your pet!

Training for the hand signal: Practice it at the same time as the spoken command.

As you utter the *sit* command, show the dog your raised right forefinger each time. It will draw the connection quickly, and soon it will sit in response to the hand signal alone.

When to practice: Direct the puppy to sit whenever the leash is to be put on or taken off. For the dog's own safety, it is important that it not race off as soon as the leash is detached. It has to remain in the sit position until you release it with an additional signal, such as *now go*. Don't make the puppy wait for more than a few seconds, however.

Practice the sit exercise at the dog's mealtimes as well. The puppy should sit in response to your command. When you set the food bowl down, your pet should wait until it has permission to eat. Invite it to do so with a certain set phrase, such as *now eat*. Make the puppy wait only a few seconds, however.

The sit command can be practiced in the course of heeling as well. Each time you stop, the dog should sit down immediately. Just before you stop, take the leash in your left hand and shorten it sharply. As you do so, give the *sit* command.

Coming on Command

One of the most important things your puppy has to learn is to come on

It is important to teach the dog to lie down.

command every time it is called, wherever it is. This lesson has to be taught in early puppyhood if you want to have a dog that can be relied on to obey later.
• Command: *here.*
• Whistle signal: Blow twice on the narrow side of the special training whistle for hunting dogs (double whistle).

How and when to practice: This is the only exercise that cannot be taught to the dog when it is on leash. For this reason, your pet should never have an opportunity not to hear the command.

It is best to begin this exercise in connection with feeding time. While you prepare its food, call the puppy's name and give the *here* command. If the dog wants to get into the kitchen any sooner than that, have another member of the family hold it firmly until your call is heard. Once the puppy is in the kitchen, greet it and shower it with praise. Once this has been successful

several times, move the session outdoors. It is best to practice in your own yard, since the puppy will be less distracted there.

Do not issue the command until you are certain that the dog will come; for example, call it when it is already moving in your direction. This situation will arise, say, when it is a few yards from reaching you and you call its name, at the same time moving away in the opposite direction. To keep from losing the connection, the puppy will follow you (see page 23). Now, while it is heading toward you, give the *here* command, and don't forget to praise your pet.

Absolutely do *not* call your dog if it is digging enthusiastically in a mouse hole, for example. In such situations, simply go to the dog and get it.

Training for the whistle signal: Drill the whistle signal after the puppy has understood the verbal command. First, issue the verbal order as described above; then, with the narrow side of the hunting dog training whistle, give the "double whistle" twice, in quick succession. Soon the puppy will react to the whistle alone.

Lying Down

This exercise will prepare the puppy later on to lie down and stay in its place until you release it again (see page 47).
• Command: *down.*
• Hand signal: Downward motion with your right hand.
• Whistle signal: Long, drawn-out tone produced with the broad side of the hunting dog training whistle.

How and when to practice: It is important that the puppy already has mastered the sit exercise (see page 36). You should never instruct your pet to stand directly from the down position; always have it sit first. Take a treat in

As its mistress holds the food bowl close to the ground and gives the here *command, this young dog cheerfully runs up to her (see Coming on Command, page 37).*

your right hand, the leash in your left. Direct the dog to sit at your left side, and squat down beside it. With your left hand, hold the leash on the ground in front of the dog, so that it is taut when the puppy is sitting. Now, holding the treat, bring your right hand downward past the dog's nose to the ground, some distance away from it. Give the *down* command simultaneously.

The puppy will lie down in order to get at the reward. Give it the treat when both its forequarters and its hindquarters are flat on the ground. Shower it with praise and stroke its back to reinforce the position even more. After a short time, direct it to sit again.

Training for the hand signal: While giving the verbal command, motion downward with your right hand. The puppy will then learn the hand signal at the same time.

Training for the whistle signal: Once the puppy has mastered the down position, you can add a whistle signal to the training.

Use the broad side of the hunting dog training whistle, which produces a trill. First, say the command or give the hand signal. That should be followed by a prolonged whistle tone. After a time, the puppy should assume the down position in response to the whistle alone.

With the same whistle tone, you will later train the dog to assume the down position at once, even at some distance from you. The whistle can act as a kind of emergency brake, for example, when the dog is in pursuit of a cat and headed for a main road. If the dog immediately drops upon hearing the whistle, its visual contact with the cat will be interrupted, and it will give up the chase. Therefore, it is important that the puppy immediately go into the down position upon hearing the whistle—for the time being, while directly next to its owner.

When practicing the down command as well, gradually discontinue the edible rewards.

Staying Alone

The dog is happiest when it is allowed to accompany its pack everywhere. Sometimes, however, there are situations in which it is preferable to leave the dog at home. For this reason it is necessary to teach the dog to spend a few hours alone as well, without howling and yowling or going after the furniture.

Being alone temporarily does not trouble a dog that has been properly

If the food bowl is held high in the air and the sit *command is given, the young dog quickly will learn to do as directed (see Sitting, page 36).*

accustomed to it. It even has a positive effect on the bond between dog and human, since the dog is all the more delighted at the return of its pack members if it has been alone for some time. Basically, however, it is contrary to a puppy's nature to be left alone.

In the wild, until the age of about four to five months, the puppies are always in the immediate vicinity of the den and never alone; therefore, you should not begin getting your pet used to being alone before it is four months old. Being left alone too early can trigger profound fear of abandonment in a puppy. That can manifest itself in howling or destructive acts, such as destroying pieces of furniture. Sometimes, disturbances of this kind appear only later, though the causes usually lie in puppyhood.

Schedule your acquisition of a dog so that someone can be with it at all times during the first few months. From that age on, young dogs are more independent, and in the wild they gradually begin to accompany the pack in pursuit of prey at this stage. They themselves do not yet start to hunt, however; usually they are made to lie down in a spot from which they can observe the goings-on.

How to practice: It is best to start getting the puppy used to being alone when it is in a fairly inactive phase—a resting phase.

Go up to your pet and say to it whatever words you plan to use every time you leave it alone from now on. You can also give it something to nibble, so that it can keep itself occupied if need be.

Now leave your home briefly—to get something out of the car, for instance. No more than two or three minutes should elapse before you return. Greet the dog briefly when you are back inside. If it sets up a steady yowl during your absence, go up to it and scold it (see Scolding, page 28).

Now leave the house again, but for only a very a short time. Gradually extend the length of time the dog stays alone. As an adult, it then will be able to stay alone for as long as half a day, should that become necessary in exceptional cases.

Riding in a Car

This is also best begun at an early age. Most dogs love to ride in cars, but to a puppy car travel is still somewhat strange and scary. The safest places for a dog, depending on its size, are the floor on the passenger side and, in vans and station wagons, the loading space in the rear. Here, it is important that the loadroom be separated from the passenger area by a special net, so that the dog does not become a projectile if an accident occurs (see drawing, page 46).

You can have your pet ride on the back seat also, but only if it is secured with a special safety belt for dogs available in some pet stores.

How to practice: In the beginning, let the puppy accompany you only on

Many dogs love to retrieve.

This boxer puppy is overjoyed to come to its owner when called (see page 37).

short rides. You should always take along a companion who can look after the dog during the trip. The dog should not be given anything to eat for several hours before the trip.

Basically, these rules apply to car travel with your dog:
- The dog is the first to get in.
- It is the last to get out.
- In the course of time, it should learn to stay seated in the car even with the doors open, until it is given permission to get out (see drawing, page 46).

Special Types of Advanced Training

A dog that is to receive special training later on needs to be made familiar with a few things while it is still a puppy. For hunting dogs, for example, these things include getting used to the water and to game and becoming familiar with retrieving. Retrieving often is a great deal of fun for other dogs as well. Consequently, here are a few tips on ways to foster your dog's ability to retrieve:
- Praise your puppy every time it brings something to you, even if it is some thoroughly unappetizing object or something that it really ought not to have.
- You should never scold it at the moment when it brings you something.
- Encourage it—by coaxing it or by pretending to run away—to bring the retrieved object to you and put it into your hand.

Good Behavior Has to Be Learned

Many people find the following habits distasteful in dogs:
- jumping up on people, and
- begging at the table.

41

If the dog is not to exhibit these behaviors later on, it has to be trained properly at an early age.

Jumping up on people: Dogs do this because of their natural behavioral patterns. Puppies and low-ranking canines greet higher-ranking pack members by licking their muzzle. That is exactly what the puppy is trying to do with you. But people are not always wearing clothing appropriate for receiving such attention, and having the front feet of a Great Dane, for instance, on one's shoulders is not everyone's cup of tea. For these reasons, you should direct your puppy's display of friendliness along more disciplined paths.

It is best to bend over to receive the puppy's greeting. Hold it firmly with both hands, and speak to it in a friendly way. As soon as it has learned to obey the *sit* command, the dog should sit when being greeted by you or your visitors.

The following method is suitable for slightly larger, boisterous young dogs. When the dog starts to jump up on you, raise your right or left knee, and catch it midchest as you correct with a firm *"No!"* That will put the dog back on the ground rather ungently. Then greet it effusively.

It is important that you follow this procedure consistently when greeting the dog, and that no one allow the dog to jump up. Otherwise, the success of this exercise is in jeopardy.

Begging at the table: The right approach is to consistently refuse to give the dog food at the table, right from the outset. If that is done, most dogs will never even think of begging. Apart from the fact that this behavior is unpleasant, the food we eat generally is not good for a dog's health.

A well-trained dog will lie peacefully in its bed or under the table while its family is eating. If you think you can break your pet of the habit of begging by giving it a tidbit now and then, you will achieve the exact opposite. In the future, a drooling or whining dog will take up its position next to the table at every meal.

Your pet naturally will exhibit this behavior not only at home, but also in friends' homes. If your pet already has formed the habit of begging and you find this annoying, consistently send it to its bed whenever you eat. Don't forget to come back and give it a release cue, however.

Playing will help keep a dog physically fit and mentally alert throughout its life. Almost all dogs love to pull and tug at objects.

Training a Companion Dog

At the age of roughly six months, your young dog already is well able to distinguish between play and work. Now it is also able to concentrate for somewhat longer periods. This is the time for puppy training to gradually turn into companion dog training. The demands are greater, the training sessions increasingly longer. The amount of time required for the exercises increases to about one hour per day. To add variety, however, continue to incorporate little breaks for play into your routine.

Drill your dog on a regular basis, and never increase the demands until it has completely understood the preceding exercises.

In the following section on training you will find all the exercises and commands that a family dog and companion dog should master. Of course, the training is also suitable for dogs that are already over six months old.

First, each individual exercise is described, from the beginners' level to the advanced level. The training section is followed by a training plan that shows you how the individual steps are arranged in a logical structure.

Basic Position

Every training session begins and ends with the basic position.

That means that at the start and the conclusion of an exercise the dog always sits at your left side, not ahead of you at an angle or behind you. The basic position helps the dog concentrate on performing the exercise.

1. Sit

The goal of the sit exercise is for the dog to sit at once on command and remain in that position until you either come to release your pet or call it off.
- Commands: *sit, sit and stay.*
- Hand signal: Raised right forefinger.

The right way to wear the collar.

First level (1a): If you have not done any puppy training with your pet, start the exercise as described on page 35. The dog is motivated through positive conditioning (see page 18). With older dogs, however, that may no longer be so effective. Then use the following method:

The dog is at your left side (basic position). Hold the dog's collar firmly with your right hand. Now, with your left hand, gently but firmly press your pet's rump down toward the ground. As you do so, give the command, *sit.* Then praise the dog.

43

At the end of this segment the dog, on leash, should immediately obey a single *sit* command. Only then should you proceed to the next segment.

Second level (1b): Next, your dog will learn, step by step, to sit and stay, waiting until you call it off or come to release it.

To begin, walk a few steps with the dog heeling (see page 35), then stop and direct your pet to sit as usual. Now say, *"Sit and stay"* and walk in front of the dog, as far as the leash—its length as yet unadjusted—will allow.

For added emphasis, show the dog the hand signal for the sit position (raised right forefinger). It is very important to make sure that the leash is sagging loosely. If the dog feels any tension, it might feel it has to stand up. This would be one of the typical errors for which the dog is not responsible.

Also make sure that the dog remains in the exact place where you told it to sit. Correct it if it moves even a few inches off that spot.

At first, have the dog sit for only a short time. Then go back to it, so that it is sitting at your left again. And don't forget the praise!

Gradually, the length of time the dog holds the sit and stay position should be increased. However, you should always go back to the dog before it gets restless and stands up. Otherwise, you have to repeat the exercise.

Third level (1c): For the next level of difficulty, lengthen the leash by one ring. Proceed exactly as described for the second level. This time, however, do not stand still in front of the dog, but walk slowly back and forth. If that works too, go on to the next level.

Fourth level (1d): Now extend the leash to its full length. After giving the

Basic position (see page 43).

The down *command (see page 47).*

sit command, slowly circle around your dog at as great a distance as possible. Again, be sure that the leash hangs loosely, and correct the dog at once if it leaves its place.

Fifth level (1e): Now lay down the leash for the first time. Proceeding as previously outlined, walk as far as possible from the dog, still holding the leash in your hand. Lay the leash on the ground and begin to walk in a circle around the dog. As you do so, keep your eye on your pet, and, if it becomes necessary, use the leash on the ground as a kind of emergency brake.

Sixth level (1f): Your pet will now be given the finishing touch as you practice with increasing levels of distraction—near a footpath or in a pedestrian area, for example. The dog should continue to be off leash at these times. For safety, however, initially you can still lay the leash on the ground.

2. Leash Training and Heeling off Leash

The dog will learn—first on a loose leash and later off leash—to stay at your left side, to watch out on its own for any changes in direction and pace, and to sit automatically whenever you stop.

• Command: *heel.*

First level (2a): Begin heeling from the basic position; that is, the dog should be sitting at your left side. Now give the command, "Heel," and set out fairly briskly. If you have not done any puppy training, try at first to motivate the dog, with a little treat held in your left hand, to stay in the right spot.

If the dog lags and hesitates, encourage it to come. If it has a tendency to pull at the leash, call it back to order by means of a sharp tug at the leash (see page 35). With a larger dog, of course, you have to apply greater force; however, only this sharp, short tug at the leash will teach the dog to heel

The basic elements of companion dog training are the *sit*, the *down*, and leash training, or heeling on leash. These exercises, which have various levels of difficulty, can be drilled when your pet is about six months old.

This dog is heeling properly (see Leash Training, page 35).

properly. If the dog is back in the right place again after the correction, relax the tension immediately. (Be sure to put the collar on the right way, see drawing, page 43). The decrease in leash tautness and your tone of voice are the dog's praise for walking properly.

With this exercise it is helpful to walk along some kind of boundary, such as a fence, with the dog between you and the fence. At first, go only short distances, and always walk straight ahead. From time to time, stop and direct the dog to sit.

If you have already practiced this with your puppy, you can begin to include curves in the training now. When you bring the exercise to a close, make sure that after its leash is removed, the dog remains in the sit position until it receives permission to stand. It should not simply race away.

Second level (2b): Once your pet has understood what *heel* means, you can start to incorporate changes in pace.

Always change from a normal tempo to a slower or faster one. Anything else would be too difficult for the dog.

Now you can also practice changes in direction, walking in zigzag lines or in figure eights. Correct the dog as needed with a tug on the leash, as described above, and don't forget to praise it for proper behavior.

Third level (2c): Next, practice turning around, that is, making a 180° turn. You can make the turn so that the dog is always kept at your left side. That way, however, it often is not so easy for the dog to tell that it's time to turn around. Consequently, there is a second option, which at first seems very complicated, but, actually, is more fluid.

Walk with your dog in the heeling position. When you are ready to make a turn, take the leash in your right hand alone and turn to the left, that is, toward the dog. Next, behind your back, transfer the leash to your left hand and walk back along your original line of march. Now your dog is at your left side again. Once you have practiced this a few times, it is quite easy.

When changing direction, make your zigzags into 90° turns to the right and left. With the right turns in particular, you should make sure that the dog moves along with you properly. If necessary, correct it with the familiar tug at the leash, but do not drag it along behind you.

Fourth level (2d): Your dog now has reached the point where it heels nicely, reacts to changes in direction and pace, and sits whenever you stop. Next you can begin to practice with a greater level of distraction, such as in town or in a park.

Fifth level (2e): Now we come to heeling off leash. That means that all the exercises from the first through the fourth level of difficulty (2a-2d) now are executed without the leash. Do not

In a station wagon or van, the rear is the best place for a dog.

begin this level, however, until the dog's execution on leash is letter-perfect; once the dog's leash is removed, there are not many ways to influence it. Continually correcting it by putting your hand on its collar is not advisable as it makes many dogs more apt to evade their owner. It also is not practicable to keep your pet in the heeling position solely by talking to it constantly. If you notice that heeling off leash is not going very well, put the dog back on leash and try the exercises again later.

3. Lying Down

This exercise has a dual purpose. First, you will be able to leave the dog somewhere in the *long down* or *down-stay* position for a quarter of an hour or more, if necessary. Second, you will be able to get the dog to stop when it is some distance away from you.
• Command: *down*.
• Hand signal: The right arm sweeps downward.
• Whistle signal: Long, drawn-out tone produced with the broad side of the whistle.

First level (3a): Proceed as for puppy training in the exercise Lying Down, described on page 38. Also use the hand signal and whistle signal at the appropriate time.

Here is an alternative training method: With the dog sitting at your left side, squat down beside it and pull the leash to the ground in front of you. Simultaneously press the dog's rump downward and say, "Down."

If your pet assumes the down position, stroke its back while repeating the command a few more times. After a short time, finish the exercise by directing the dog to sit once more. If you have taught your dog the down command while it was still a puppy, you now can increase the length of time it has to remain in the down position.

Second level (3b): Following, step by step, are the exercises for the down position. In the first phase, proceed analogously to the sit and stay exercise (see page 44). From the basic position, have the dog assume the down position, then step out a little in front of it.

As with the sit exercises, here too you have to make sure that the leash always sags loosely and that the dog does not leave its place. The way it lies there is irrelevant; it can lie on one side or turn from one side to the other, as long as it does not get up or scoot along on its belly. When you come back to get the dog, approach it so that it is lying at your left side. Now it should stay in the down position until you tell it to sit.

Third level (3c): Lengthen the leash by one ring and walk back and forth in front of the dog while it is in the down position.

Fourth level (3d): Now extend the leash to its full length. After giving the sit command, slowly walk in a circle around your dog, at as great a distance as possible. Again, make especially sure that leash is sagging, and correct the dog immediately if it leaves its place.

Fifth level (3e): Lay the leash on the ground.

Sixth level (3f): If everything went well, you can now practice with a greater level of distraction—in the park, for example—and off leash. Gradually extend the length of time the dog spends in the down position to several minutes.

4. Lying Down, Out of Sight

Once your dog stays in the down position while you are in its range of vision, it is ready to learn gradually to maintain that position while you are out of sight as well. For reinforcement, you can make it a habit to put a piece of your clothing next to the dog when

During training it is important to structure the exercises systematically and to avoid overtaxing the dog. Raise your demands only when the dog has fully mastered the preceding exercises.

Sit and stay. *The dog is learning to remain in the sit position while you move away.*

it is down. Then your pet will have a familiar smell nearby, and staying in its position will be easier for it.

• Command: *down and stay.*

First level (4a): Your dog is already used to remaining in the down position while it can see you. Now, after using the command, "Down and stay" to have it lie down somewhere in your home, start walking through the rooms. That way, the dog will catch a glimpse of you now and then, and in between, you will be out of sight. Keep an eye on your pet, so that you can correct it if need be. After about two minutes, come back to release it.

Second level (4b): Put the dog into the down position as usual, inside your home or in the yard, and go out of sight. The dog should not see you, but you should be able to observe it. Come back for it after a few minutes.

If it gets up before that, go to it quickly and put it into the down position again, with a clear command. If possible, briefly go away once more. If the dog does not stay in the down position when alone, put it into the position again while you remain in view.

Third level (4c): Now keep lengthening the amount of time, until the dog stays in the down position for about ten to 15 minutes. Then direct it to drop somewhere other than your home or yard—in a vacant lot or a field, for example—but without incorporating any distractions just yet.

Fourth level (4d): Once your dog will stay in the down position alone for several minutes without difficulty, you can begin to train it to lie down and stay when there are distractions. Put it into the down position at the edge of a

At the preliminary levels of the *sit and stay* (see page 43) and *down and stay* (see page 48) exercises, the dog remains on leash. It is important in these exercises that the leash always sag loosely.

Down and stay. *The dog is learning to remain in the down position (see Lying Down, page 47).*

path, for example, where a number of walkers pass by, and hide behind a tree.

5. Coming on Command

Now your dog will learn to come to you happily, in response to the *here* command, or the double whistle tone (see page 38), and to assume the *sit* position in front of you. Upon hearing the *heel* command, it then will walk around your back, so that it once again is sitting at his or her left side.

• Commands: *here, come,* and *heel.*
• Whistle signal: Two short tones produced with the narrow side of the hunting dog training whistle (double whistle).

Note: If you have gone through the puppy training program with your dog, you will have already taught it the meaning of the *here* command, (see page 37). Now all you have to do is teach the dog to combine coming when called with sitting exactly in front of you. Make sure that this exercise is executed precisely and in its entirety whenever you use the recall command during a walk. That is the only way to get the dog accustomed to coming all the way to you each time.

First level (5a): Start the more advanced exercise when your pet has learned to stay in the down position while you are out of sight. Moving in a straight line, walk away as far as the leash allows, but the leash still has to sag loosely. Turn toward the dog and wait a few seconds before giving the *here* command. If the dog doesn't know the command yet and hesitates, coax it while pulling gently on the leash. If the dog starts moving toward you, quickly shorten the leash to keep it from going past you. Once it reaches you, put it into the *sit in front* position; that is, it should sit directly in front of you and look at you. During the initial phase you can hold a treat in your hand at about stomach height, to help make the *sit in front* easier for your dog. Finish the exercise as described above.

Second level (5b): The next step is to execute the exercise described in the first level, off leash. Make sure the dog doesn't race off at once when you turn around to face it. If your pet is inclined to do just that, let it wait one or two minutes before you recall it with the *here* command. To reinforce the *sit,* you can come to the dog to release it occasionally, instead of calling it.

Third level (5c): Now get your dog used to the double whistle, if you didn't already do so while it was a puppy. Leave it on leash at the beginning, until it has understood the whistle. First give the command verbally, and, right after that, blow twice in succession on the narrow side of the whistle.

Good behavior is called for on public transportation. However in the United States, only seeing eye dogs are allowed on public transportation.

Fourth level (5d): Now whistle to recall the dog off leash. Don't forget to finish the exercise properly with the heel command.

Fifth level (5e): Alternate the verbal command and the whistle signal, and practice the recall while increasing the level of distraction. Gradually increase the distance between you and your pet.

6. Dropping, at a Distance

This exercise will provide you with a kind of emergency brake for use when the dog is on dangerous wrong paths. Only a whistle signal is used. The dog has to drop into the down position as soon as it hears the whistle.

Especially at relatively great distances, a whistle is far more penetrating than a verbal command.

• Whistle signal: Long, drawn-out tone produced with the broad side of the hunting dog training whistle (trill).

First level (6a): From the basic position at your left side, the dog now can assume the down position in response to a verbal command. Next give it the down command followed by a whistle signal. At first, practice this from the basic position (see page 43), then from slow heeling (see page 45). If the dog is already familiar with the whistle signal, omit the verbal command. It is important that the dog drop into the down position quickly. If it is slow to react, help it along by pressing down on its nape.

Second level (6b): If the dog immediately drops at your side when it hears the whistle, practice the same exercise off leash.

Third level (6c): If that is working well too, whistle the dog into the down position when it is not distracted and is about six to 12 yards (2–3 m) away from you. For this exercise, it is important that you be able to reach the dog quickly if it fails to obey immediately.

Fourth level (6d): Now increase the distance gradually. However, do not choose a greater distance unless the dog can be counted on to lie down immediately at a lesser distance. Only when the dog has completely mastered this exercise do you have a guarantee that it can be made to stop and drop in an emergency.

Fifth level (6e): As its level of mastery increases, you can whistle your pet down when its attention is being distracted. With dogs that are not high-spirited or have little instinct to hunt and chase, it is sufficient to train them until they will sit as soon as they hear the trill.

Your Dog as a Recreational Partner

Many dog owners also love engaging in sports in their free time. The dog should be included often, especially in such activities as biking and jogging.

Note: Not all dog breeds are suited for these types of stresses; therefore, you need to get the requisite information before acquiring a dog (see page 56).

Running Beside Your Bicycle

Starting at the age of roughly six months, a dog that is normally developed can be slowly accustomed to run alongside a bicycle—at the outset, for no more than a few minutes.

The dog should run at the right side of the bicycle—that is, between the curb and the bike. Use a special command for this purpose, such as *right* or *bike*. It has to be clearly distinguishable from *heel*.

First, push the bicycle while you lead the dog, on leash, next to it. The bike should be between you and the dog. Don't put the collar on the same way you do for leash training; here the ring of the collar has to be on the left side of the dog's neck (the dog has to run at the right of the bike). Just as when heeling, incidentally, the dog should not be allowed to mark with urine once you are underway, whether it is off or on leash, when following the *bike* command. That would show disdain for you personally, that is, for the superdog. Also, it could be very dangerous for you if the dog suddenly were to drag you, along with the bike, into the bushes. For this reason, never wrap the leash tightly around your hand.

When pushing the bike goes well, you can start riding slowly. Just as when doing leash training (see page 45), start by moving straight ahead, then incorporate some curves and change the pace—first faster, then slower. If you stop, the dog should sit down immediately. First it should do that in response to the sit command; later on, that will happen even without the command.

Don't ask too much of your dog. Start with short rides of about ten minutes and lengthen them gradually.

Keep an eye on the pace. The dog is supposed to trot, not gallop.

As a Companion when You Jog

Many dogs enjoy jogging as well. This is nothing more than heeling at a run (see page 46). Pet stores now offer special jogging leashes that you fasten around your middle. Here, too, the same rule applies: Don't ask too much of the dog, but build up its endurance gradually by increasing the pace steadily over a number of days. In an area with little traffic—and if the dog has an appropriate level of obedience—you can let it run off leash both when biking and when jogging.

Since a dog always wants to be with its family, it enjoys taking part in its owner's recreational activities as well. Before acquiring a pedigreed dog, however, find out whether it is suited for the stresses of athletic activity.

Going for a Walk with Your Dog

The more obedient your dog is, the more freedom you can grant it during a walk.

In areas populated with game, as well as during the hatching times and breeding periods of wildlife, do not allow the dog to run into meadows or fields. A dog that cannot be depended upon to obey when it is off leash has to be leashed in such areas.

Stray dogs certainly are no rarity anywhere. There are dog owners who let their pets stray in order to save themselves the bother of taking them for a walk. But a dog also can stray when it gets too little attention at home or has too strong a sex drive.

If the dog's sex drive is very pronounced, castration is advisable. In other cases, it helps to spend more time with the dog, engage in plenty of activities with it, and show it ample affection.

Stray dogs easily can place themselves and others in danger. For example, they can cause serious traffic accidents, be accidentally shot by a hunter when chasing game, and at times behave unpredictably toward other dogs and humans as well.

Encountering Other Dogs

Basically, it is very beneficial for a dog to meet other members of its species when out for a walk with you (see page 24). When that happens, however, follow these ground rules:

• If strange dogs meet and their dispositions are relatively normal, it is best for them to be off leash. They can then sniff at each other to their heart's content and

The *180° turn* is a component of the exercise "Leash training and heeling off leash" (see third level, page 46). This exercise looks complicated, but is quite simple after some training. Your motions should be as fluid as possible.

Take the leash in your right hand . . .

. . . transfer it to your left hand as you turn

become acquainted. Either a game will develop, or each dog will go its own way.

• If the dogs take a dislike to each other, the situation no longer looks so benign (see HOW-TO: Dog Language, "Threatening Behavior," page 14). The best course of action is for you and the other dog owner to keep moving in opposite directions and to call your dogs.

• If your dog ever gets involved in a fight, don't try to intervene! If the dogs' dispositions are normal, they usually will separate on their own after a short while. If not, the owners can try to grab their pets simultaneously, by their hind legs, and separate them in that way.

• It is usually not a good situation when dogs meet and one is on leash while the other is off; a fight can easily be the result. When a dog on leash approaches you and your dog, leash your pet as well.

• If both dogs are on leash when they meet, chances are nothing will happen. However, you should make it a rule never to let strange dogs on leash get too close. Male dogs, in particular, often feel strong when they are on leash. In addition, the dogs could get their leashes tangled while playing, and that predicament often leads to a fight.

. . . and continue heeling.

Plan for Training a Companion Dog

The individual stages of the training program are designated with capital letters in this table. The exercises given for each stage were described step by step in the preceding material. The exercises are arranged in a logical sequence, and they constitute a training program that offers your pet plenty of variety.

The exercises for each stage can be learned by your dog in about one or two weeks, depending on the amount of time you invest in the training. Never proceed to the next stage until the dog has mastered all the preceding ones. Each time, practice not only the new lesson, but the previous ones as well.

My tip: Several dog owners and their pets can get together in small groups to practice the exercises (see photo, page 29).

Stage	Exercise	Objective
Stage A	1a, sit (see page 43)	Dog learns to sit on command (basic position; dog sits at left).
	2a heel (see page 45)	Dog heels straight ahead; if you stop, it sits on command.
	3a down (see page 47)	Dog learns to go from basic position into down position.
Stage B	1b, sit and stay (see page 44)	Dog stays seated, on leash, while you stand in front of it. Leash is not lengthened and sags loosely.
	2b, heel (see page 46)	In heeling, incorporate stops, changes in pace, and curves.
	3b, down and stay (see page 47)	Dog, on leash, stays in down position while you stand in front of it
Stage C	1c, sit and stay (see page 44)	Dog, on leash, stays in sit position while you walk back and forth in front of it, with the leash suddenly lengthened.
	2c, heel (see page 46)	In heeling, include 180° turn and change of direction.
	3c, down and stay (see page 47)	On leash, dog stays in down position while you walk back and forth in front of it
Stage D	1d, sit and stay (see page 44)	On leash, dog stays in sit position while you circle around it, with the leash at full length.
	2d, heel (see page 46)	Now practice leash training in busier surroundings.
	3d, down and stay (see page 47)	On leash, dog stays in down position while you circle around it, with the leash at full length.
Stage E	1e, sit and stay (see page 45)	On leash, dog stays in sit position; the leash lies on the ground as you circle around your pet.
	3e, down and stay (see page 47)	Proceed as for 1e, but with the dog in the down position.
	5a, here (see page 49)	On leash, dog sits the full length of the leash away from you. On command it comes to you and sits in front of you.

Stage	Exercise	Objective
		At the *heel* command, it walks around behind you and sits at your left side.
Stage F	1f, sit and stay (see page 45)	Off leash and with distraction, the dog stays alone in the down position. You stay in sight.
	2e, heel (off leash) (see page 46)	Dog learns to heel when off leash.
	3f, down and stay (see page 47)	Off leash and with distraction, dog stays in down position. You stay in sight.
Stage G	6a, down (on whistle) (see page 50)	On leash, dog learns to lie down from the basic position and from slow walking to heel, upon hearing the whistle.
	4a, down and stay (out of sight at times) (see page 48)	In your home, put the dog into down position and walk around from room to room so that you are sometimes visible, sometimes not.
	5b, here (on leash) (see page 50)	Do this exercise as described for Stage E/5a, but with the dog off leash.
Stage H	6b, down (on whistle) (see page 50)	From heeling off leash, the dog is put into down position by means of a whistle signal.
	4b, down and stay (out of sight) (see page 48)	Dog learns to stay in down position for a short time with you out of sight.
	5c, here (with double whistle) (see page 50)	On leash, dog learns to come to you upon hearing double whistle.
Stage I	6c, down (on whistle) (see page 50)	At sound of whistle, dog goes into down position when several yards away from you.
	4c, down and stay (out of sight) (see page 48)	Dog gradually learns to stay in down position up to ten minutes with you out of sight.
	5d, here (with double whistle) (see page 50)	Off leash also, dog comes at once upon hearing whistle.
Stage J	6d, down (on whistle) (see page 51)	The dog can be brought to a halt at increasingly long distances.
	4d, down and stay (out of sight) (see page 48)	With distraction, dog is put into down position with you out of sight.
	6e, down (on whistle) (see page 51)	At varying distances, dog is put into down position with whistle, when distractions are present.

Dog Breeds and What Makes Them Special

If you want to get a dog, you are faced with the predicament of choosing among almost 400 breeds.

Dog breeds can be roughly divided into the following groups: working dogs, sporting dogs, hounds, terriers, toys, non-sporting dogs, and herding dogs.

Within each of these groups there are breeds that have varying characteristics and needs. Many are suitable as family pets or for first-time dog owners. Others—some sporting dogs and herding dogs, for example—continue even today to be used primarily as working dogs. Such breeds often are not easy to keep unless provided with appropriate activities. Lack of activity, in turn, can result in the inhibition of natural instincts, and that has the potential to create behavior problems. Some dogs, owing to their characteristic traits, are not suitable for beginners, but need owners with experience in owning dogs. In this chapter I would like to make you aware of some special features of the various breeds.

When selecting a breed, be sure to get exact information about the needs and peculiarities of each individual breed. It is equally important to be clear in your own mind about what you expect of the dog.

Working and Herding Dogs

All the breeds classified as working or herding dogs have been bred for a certain purpose. For example, there are dogs used in herding work whose task it is to watch over herds of sheep or cattle. The Shetland sheepdog is one such dog. There are typical watchdogs or dogs used in protection work, such as the German shepherd, and sled dogs, such as Siberian huskies.

Some working dogs are entirely suitable as family dogs also, but breeds in this group can be kept properly only if they are allowed to do real work.

Good family dogs include, for example, boxers, Old English sheepdogs, Bernese mountain dogs, and collies.

Not good candidates, however, especially for novice dog owners, are breeds that are bred primarily to be trained as guard dogs or police dogs. These include, for example, Rottweilers and Doberman pinschers. Nature has provided them with a certain, sometimes excessive, amount of protective and fighting instincts.

The border collie, frequently touted as an ideal family dog, is becoming increasingly fashionable in Europe. Actually, however, the border collie is a working dog *par excellence*, probably the best herd dog of all (see photo, right). The role of family pet usually is not sufficiently fulfilling for it and the results can range from behavior problems to aggressiveness.

The same is true of the Siberian husky. It feels happiest in a pack of other huskies at the front of a dog sled.

Sporting Dogs

This is a large group. It includes such breeds as retrievers, setters, and spaniels. In general these are friendly dogs, since they were not intended for use in guarding or protection work, but were bred to assist hunters. Moreover, the sporting dog breeds (gun dogs, shooting dogs, bird dogs) are usually quite eager to

A border collie, an excellent sheepdog, at work.

learn and intelligent, since for the most part they are required to perform tasks independently. In addition, most of these breeds have a great need for exercise.

Among sporting dogs, too, there are some breeds that are better suited as family pets and others that can lead a happy life only with a hunter. Even the family hunting dogs, however, need a great deal of exercise.

Good family dogs are cocker spaniels, golden and Labrador retrievers, and setters. Most hunting dogs have a more or less pronounced hunting instinct and consequently should reach a good level of obedience, so that they do not have to be kept on leash at all times in woods and fields.

Hounds

Hounds actually are hunting dogs. They do not hunt with their nose, how-

ever, but with their eyes. These dogs have an enormous need to be in motion, and that makes them difficult to keep properly as ordinary family pets.

In addition, the nature of hounds is different from that of other breeds. They tend to be restrained and reserved, and they cannot be trained in the same way as a hunting dog or a working dog, for example.

Most suitable as family dogs are dachshunds, Basset hounds, and Afghan hounds. Other hounds should be considered only if you can provide them with an opportunity for enough exercise.

Terriers

This group includes about 28 different breeds. Most terrier breeds were originally employed as so-called earth dogs (Latin *terra* = "earth") for hunting foxes and badgers that had gone to earth. Consequently, they all are more or less combative, courageous, high-spirited, and very alert.

Today, most terriers are kept solely as companion dogs. Only the German hunting terrier and the smooth-haired fox terrier are still seen relatively often in hunting use.

Among the terriers also there are breeds that are easier to keep and breeds that are not suitable for beginners.

Good companion and family dogs include miniature schnauzers, Boston terriers, and airedales, to name only a few. Among the best-known terriers surely are the Yorkshire terrier (Yorkie) and the West Highland white terrier (Westie). Both breeds quite incorrectly have the reputation of being lapdogs. In fact, they possess the typical terrier traits and are anything but lapdogs. With the West Highland white terrier in particular, which has become a very trendy pet, problems caused by aggressive behavior are becoming increasingly common.

Unsuitable as family dogs—especially for inexperienced dog owners—are the bull terrier varieties.

Non-Sporting (or Companion) Dogs

This group includes all the breeds that for a good many years have been kept exclusively for companionship. A well-known representative of this group of breeds is the Dalmatian. It makes a very good family dog, but needs plenty of exercise.

Other breeds that are excellently suited as companion and family dogs are poodles, in its four sizes, and bichon frises. Most of the small and toy dog breeds can be considered companion dogs. A special feature of these breeds is a large, round head, which gives them an eternally puppylike appearance and makes them popular as lapdogs. For dogs in this category, however, their appearance often has great disadvantages. Frequently, the females are no longer able to whelp normally; their puppies have to be delivered by cesarean section because their heads are much too large.

Dogs and Children

Children frequently yearn for a dog. We have long had scientific proof that owning a dog can have a positive effect on a child's development, because it inculcates a sense of responsibility and duty. Also, the dog functions as a confidant and a playmate for the child.

However, there is a long way to go before one sees the positive effects that a dog can have on a child. First, the dog must be given an opportunity to develop in a normal, healthy way. Here the adult members of the family have to become involved.

The dog will require, on a regular basis, food, affection, grooming, exercise, and training. An adult will have to find time for these needs as keeping up with such a list of chores is too much to ask of a child.

When selecting a breed, parents need to proceed carefully. In general, we can say that dog breeds that have a high stimulus threshold (absolute threshold)—that is, they are not given to aggressive behavior—are more suitable for children than other breeds. Behavioral research, however, assumes that friendly behavior toward children is less a question of the dog's breed than of its individual proclivities.

In general, small breeds are not suitable, especially for younger children, as they are more apt to feel threatened by somewhat rougher handling, and react accordingly.

The relationship between the dog and the child is something that parents should keep a watchful eye on. Naturally a child has to learn how to properly treat a dog and to understand that a dog is not a toy. But it is inevitable that small children, in particular, will accidentally step on a paw or a tail, or seize a dog's coat or ear somewhat roughly. A children's dog should be so robust and tolerant that it is unruffled in such situations and does not react in panic or, even worse, behave aggressively.

Don't get a puppy, I suggest, if there is a child under three or four years old in the family. Puppies play quite boisterously and, use their extremely sharp little teeth. In addition, they like to jump up on people, which can be frightening for small children.

Keep in mind: Even a dog that is extremely good with children is not a machine, therefore, you should *never* leave a small child alone with a dog.

A spaniel trained to hunt can be depended upon to retrieve game that has been shot.

Index

A properly trained dog will also accept other pets as members of its pack. Often, real friendships will even develop.

Useful Addresses and Literature

Dog Clubs and Organizations

The addresses of local dog clubs and organizations can be obtained from the American Kennel Club and similar organizations.

Dog Training Courses

In various parts of the United States, dog clubs conduct scientifically based "puppy play days" and training courses. Please contact the American Kennel Club and similar organizations for more information.

Liability Insurance

Many insurance companies now offer liability insurance policies for dogs. Ask for more information at your local veterinary office.

Health Insurance for Dogs

Ask your veterinarian for information.

Also contact Veterinary Pet Insurance (call toll-free: 1-800-872-7387).

Registration of Dogs

[Central Pet Registry]

If you want to protect your pet from dognappers and from death in an experimental lab, you can register it here. There is a small charge for listing your dog or for making a computer search, should it be reported missing. For more information, contact the American Kennel Club.

Kennel Clubs

American Kennel Club
51 Madison Avenue
New York, New York 10038

Australian Kennel Club
Royal Show Ground
Ascot Vale
Victoria, Australia

Canadian Kennel Club
2150 Bloor Street
Toronto, Ontario Canada M6540

Irish Kennel Club
41 Harcourt Street
Dublin, 2, Ireland

The Kennel Club
1–4 Clargis Street, Picadilly
London, W7Y 8AB
England

New Zealand Kennel Club
P.O. Box 523
Wellington, 1
New Zealand

Information and Printed Material

American Boarding Kennel
   Association
   4575 Galley Road, Suite 400A
   Colorado Springs, Colorado 80915
(Publishes lists of approved boarding kennels)

American Society for the Prevention
   of Cruelty to Animals (ASPCA)
   441 East 92nd Street
   New York, New York 10128

American Veterinary Medical
   Association
   930 North Meacham Road
   Schaumburg, Illinois 60173

Fédération Cynologique
   Internationale
   Rue Leopold II
   Thuin, Belgium

Gaines TWT
   P.O. Box 8172
   Kankakee, Illinois 60901
(Publishes "Touring with Towser," a directory of hotels and motels that accommodate guests with dogs.)

Humane Society of the United States
   (HSUS)
   2100 L Street NW
   Washington, DC 20037

Books for Additional Reading

In addition to the most recent edition of the official publication of the American Kennel Club, *The Complete Dog Book*, published by Howell Book House, New York, other suggestions include:

Alderton, David. *The Dog Care Manual.* Barron's Educational Series, Inc., Hauppauge, New York: 1986.

Baer, Edith. *Communicating with Your Dog.* Barron's Educational Series, Inc., Hauppauge, New York: 1989.

————. *How To Teach Your Old Dog New Tricks.* Barron's Educational Series, Inc., Hauppauge, New York: 1991.

Klever, Ulrich. *The Complete Book of Dog Care.* Barron's Educational Series, Inc., Hauppauge, New York: 1989.

Pinney, Chris C. *Guide to Home Pet Grooming.* Barron's Educational Series, Inc., Hauppauge, New York: 1990.

Ullmann, Hans. *The New Dog Handbook.* Barron's Educational Series, Inc., Hauppauge, New York: 1984.

Wrede, Barbara. *Civilizing Your Puppy.* Barron's Educational Series, Inc., Hauppauge, New York: 1992.

About the Author

Katharina Schlegl-Kofler has long been interested in the appropriate care and training of dogs. She has owned retrievers for many years and is the author of a book on this breed. For 15 years she has conducted training courses for dogs of all breeds.

About the Photographer

Christine Steimer has been a free-lance photographer since 1985, when she began to specialize in animal photography. Since that time she has done work for the German magazine, *Das Tier*.

About the Illustrator

Renate Holzner works as a free-lance illustrator in Regensburg, Germany. Her wide repertoire ranges from line drawings through illustrations in the style of photographic realism to computer graphics.

Acknowledgments

The author and the publishers of this book are grateful to Dr. Dorit Feddersen-Petersen and Ms. Astrid Ebenhoch for their kind permission to photograph the work of training groups affiliated with the Committee to Combat Leash Laws and Hostility toward Animals.

The Cover Photos

Front cover: Modern dog training is based on gentle training methods.

Back cover: One appropriate way to scold a dog.

All inquiries should be addressed to:
Barron's Educational Series, Inc.
250 Wireless Boulevard
Hauppauge, NY 11788

International Standard Book No. 0-8120-9592-8

Library of Congress Catalog Card No. 95-50335

Library of Congress Cataloging-in-Publication Data
Schlegl-Kofler, Katharina.
   [*Erziehung mit Herz und Verstand*. English]
   Educating your dog with love and understanding : the basics of appropriate training for all dogs, from puppyhood through adulthood / Katharina Schlegl-Kofler ; color photos by Cristine Steimer ; drawings by Renate Holzner ; consulting editor, Matthew M. Vriends.
        p.   cm.
   Includes bibliographical references (p.   ) and index.
   ISBN 0-8120-9592-8
   1. Dogs—Training. I. Vriends, Matthew M., 1937–   . II. Title.
SF431.S3413   1996
636.7'0887—dc20   95-50335
                                                                     CIP

Printed in Hong Kong

987654321

Important Note

This pet owner's manual tells the reader how to train a dog. The author and the publisher consider it important to point out that the guidelines given in the book are meant primarily for normally developed dogs from a good breeder—that is, dogs of excellent physical health and good character. Anyone who adopts a fully grown dog should be aware that the animal has already been substantially influenced by human beings. The new owner should watch the animal carefully, including its behavior toward humans, and, if possible, meet the previous owner. If the dog comes from a shelter, it may be possible to get some information on the dog's background and peculiarities there.

There are dogs that, as a result of bad experiences with humans, behave in an unnatural way or even tend to bite. Only people who have experience with dogs should own such an animal. Even well-trained and carefully supervised dogs sometimes damage property or even cause accidents. It is in the owner's interest to be adequately insured against such eventualities, and we strongly urge all dog owners to purchase a liability policy that covers their pet.

What looks quite easy and natural in this photo is the result of long, regular training. Three dogs in a combined *stay* position. With great concentration, they wait for the trainer's instructions.